10 Weeks to a Better Retail Operation

Published 2012

By
Discovery-Based Retail
© 2012 Philip H. Mitchell & Gary A. Petz

(888) 292-6531

Without limiting the rights under copyright reserved above, no part of this publication may be reproduced, stored in or introduced into a retrieval system or transmitted, in any form, by any means (electronic, mechanical, photocopying, recording, or otherwise), without the prior written permission of the copyright owner and the above publisher of this book.

Publisher's Note

The scanning, uploading, and distribution of this book via the Internet or via any other means without the permission of the publisher is illegal and punishable by law. Please purchase only authorized electronic editions, and do not participate in or encourage electronic piracy of copyrighted materials. Your support of the author's rights is appreciated.

Disclaimer

The writing in this book is for information purposes only. Neither the authors nor the publisher nor any of the employees or subcontractors make any warranty, expressed or implied, or assumes an legal liability or responsibility for the accuracy, completeness or usefulness of any data, information, method, product or process disclosed in this document.

Published
2012

10 Weeks to a Better Retail Operation

DISCOVERY-BASED

10 Weeks To a Better Retail Operation!

Learn How to Quickly Improve Your Store.

Philip H. Mitchell

And

Gary Petz

10 Weeks to a Better Retail Operation

Contents

Introduction 7
Understanding the Six Ps of Differentiation 13
1. Don't Judge a Book by its Cover 21
2. Interior Layout and Environment 31
3. Merchandising and Other Stuff 41
4. Marketing, Branding and Reaching Out 57
5. Employees and Teamwork 87
6. Scratching a Niche 107
7. Pricing and Margin 119
8. Short-term and long-term planning 135
9. Watching and working the numbers 141
10. Systems, processes and tying it altogether 151
Final thoughts 157

10 Weeks to a Better Retail Operation

Introduction

Back in 2008 we set out to write a book that would help people in the industry in which we work most frequently—hardware stores and home centers. What we learned early on, after writing *Discovery-Based Retail*, was that the things that we were trying to teach went far beyond the boundaries of just two industries. In fact, it was interesting and gratifying to have the book embraced by so many people operating different types of stores.

I guess it shouldn't have been that much of a surprise. After all, things that work well in one industry often translate to another and, in fact, many people make the argument that looking outside of your own industry is a great way to become exposed to new ideas and strategies.

I'm one who embraces "common sense"...if it makes sense to me I'm all about trying a new idea. In fact, in conversations, whether one on one or in presentations to large groups, I'll often ask others to consider contrarian ideas. I then ask them to evaluate as to whether the suggestions seem like common sense to them. If the ideas pass the common sense test, then I suggest that they move forward and try them. That might be a good guideline for you and for reading this book too.

Not all ideas are good. I'll certainly throw mine into that pile, but, remember this: a store that isn't trying to improve is D.O.A (Dead on Apathy). I've noticed that once an owner or manager loses his passion, D.O.A. gradually or not so gradually slips in.

Look around, observe the stores in which you shop, filter the experiences yourself and maybe you'll recognize some stores that you would characterize as D.O.A.

One of the disheartening parts of retail is that you're never at the top of the hill. There are always new items, new employees, new technologies, new competitors and the list goes on. But that said, the assuring part is that even though things do change, and change quickly, there are also some tried and true methods and systems that are as solid today as they were twenty years ago.

Some time ago I wrote an article titled "Retail Genetics" that appeared in some e-magazines. I'm sure it's still out there in cyberspace somewhere (search Google for Retail Genetics and Phil Mitchell, if you're interested). In that article I made the argument that just like many of our individual personal characteristics are the result of our genetics...the DNA of our parents, their parents etc... our daily managerial actions are influenced by those who trained and mentored us.

If you agree with that then it is time we ask ourselves some questions: Is it possible that we were taught wrong? Could it be that things have changed so much that what was once important and relevant is no longer so? Or, are the old teachings while perhaps still relevant, given new circumstances, now incomplete? I think that you will agree that the answer to at least a couple of these questions might be yes.

If it sounds like I'm going to make an argument for broad-sweeping change, well not really. I guess that would depend on where your operation is today and there's no way for me to know that. I'm going to guide you through some mental exercises and as I said before, if they resonate as common-sense, then, at the very least we'll have you thinking about things in a new way.

In addition to that, we're going to review some of the most basic lessons. It is our hope that this combination of introducing new thoughts and reviewing old ones will stir up your brain, cause it to be more receptive, and encourage you to be more creative as you move forward.

I know this for a fact. Many store types are steeped in tradition; for example, things as simple as what departments constitute a hardware store are usually just a matter of "what has always been". But what if you were to examine and find that one of those traditional departments just doesn't work in your operation? Would you be better off to continue to try to improve it or would you benefit from dumping it and taking on a non-traditional category that might work? You would have to break free of the traditional model, wouldn't you? And if you were to do that would your store no longer be a hardware store? How would you feel about that?

As I mentioned earlier, the same things would hold true with whatever you're selling. I use the traditional hardware store for example only. Whatever your store type, there was probably a model you were imitating when you started the store, or whenever, whomever started the store. Does it still make sense? Is it tuned to perfection and producing at its maximum potential? Hopefully these are all thought provoking questions that will cause you to think and examine more closely.

OK, here's a quick note of who this book is for. During my career I've had the privilege of learning from a number of great people. I have had the opportunity to work for large companies and small ones. It occurred to me one day that the managers of chain stores have a tremendous advantage over singularly owned stores.

I worked for the TG&Y Company, an early day discount retailer that had many stores spread across the country, back in the late 70s. Back then we would be sent instructions...down to pictures of side counters, requirements for end caps, maintenance schedules and budget numbers. These programs were all monitored each month, and the requirements and directions went on and on.

Since then I have started visualizing these corporate systems as "giant thinking heads" disseminating information, instructions and disciplines to the stores beneath. Independently owned stores do not have their own personal giant thinking head. They are left to their own design which can be either good or bad.

Back to the question of who is this book is for. It's not for the large chains although small ones could benefit greatly. It is for those of you out there going it alone, depending on advice from wherever and whomever you can get it.

10 Weeks to a Better Retail Operation is more than a title, it is my goal for you. Unfortunately, my goal for you won't mean much. But your goal for yourself and for your store, well now, that's a horse of a different color. Will you entertain change? If so, then you'll benefit from this book.

If I come off as a "Mr. Know-it-all-smarty-britches", let me apologize for that in advance for it's not in keeping with my character. I do believe I have a way of framing things in a context that can lead to new ways of thinking and for that I am grateful. When you're done reading the book, perhaps you will agree.

If you find this book interesting you will probably read it through before you choose which of the ideas to act on. That's fine, but if you truly want to improve your operation it will take some investment of effort. That is the reason that I suggest you take one chapter at a time, work with the ideas, each for at least a week, and if you do, then I feel quite comfortable that you will be only *10 Weeks to a Better Retail Operation*.

10 Weeks to a Better Retail Operation

Understanding the Six Ps of Differentiation

Before you have finished reading this book you may tire of me beating you over the head reinforcing how important differentiation is to your business. It is, you know. In fact, I will be bold and say that differentiation is perhaps the most critical component of your store's, or any store's success.

Imagine a field of yellow flowers… any kind you choose, but they must all be the same. In that field of yellow flowers if you were to examine them close enough perhaps you could pick out small differences, but for the most part, each yellow flower is just like the rest. If we were standing together in your field of yellow flowers and I asked you to pick your favorite, it would be hard to do. Remember they all look about the same.

Now take a leap with me and imagine you are a prospective customer and each of those yellow flowers represents a choice of where you can spend your hard-earned money. Because there are no distinguishing factors to speak of, your decision would be difficult…right?

But now let's say that in the middle of the field of yellow flowers is a bright red rose. If I asked you to pick the flower that stands out, I'd give you odds that you'd pick the red one...almost all of us would. Why? It is because it's different and, therefore, it demands our attention.

There are a number of ways that you could make your store different from your competitors'. Some of those ways would be good, some would probably be bad. In fact, it might seem that the number of ways in which you could differentiate your store would be infinite, and that wouldn't be far from the truth. *But there are a limited number of differentiating categories.*

We teach that there are only 6 categories within which you can separate your retail operation. Every distinguishing factor you might think of would fall within one of these categories. And this is very important because an owner can quite manageably think and formulate strategies within the context of 6 groups. But the almost infinite number of ways in which you might differentiate your store without the boundaries of categories, would be something, I think, akin to herding cats.

So get out your highlighter, if you haven't already, and paint these puppies yellow or green or whatever your color of choice.

6 PS OF DIFFERENTIATION

1. **PROXIMITY**
2. **PEOPLE**
3. **PRESENTATION**
4. **PROMOTION**
5. **PRICING**
6. **PRODUCTS**

I put proximity first for a few different reasons. Proximity has everything to do with your store's location and more explicitly, with your store's location in relationship to its target customers. Often a store wins the battle of differentiation simply because it is the most convenient. Its proximity is such that it attracts customers simply because of where it is located and the convenience it offers.

The second reason I put Proximity first is because it is the "P" that is least subject to change, short of relocating. Nonetheless, it is critical to understand that when people are deciding which yellow flower to pick, or in our case, which store to shop, the one that is the nearest often gets the nod.

But here is the reality which we face today. Often the competitor that is most convenient, is not the one that resides 2 miles down the road but, rather, somewhere on another coast. Its front door is not of oak but of digits. Cyberspace and e-commerce are game changers and there's no doubt about that. While you're tucked away in your nice warm bed, one of your customers, possibly in his underwear, or heaven forbid, even less, may be placing an order for a what-cha-ma-call-it on the computer in his bedroom from ...well, you fill in the address. It's an item you sell every day, maybe even for less, who knows? But the proximity effect, in this case, is the store that's just down the hall.

While many small or mid-sized retailers have internet presences, most do not have online e-commerce. That could change, but when one enters the realm of cyber space they do battle with inter-galactic bullies. The bullies are often huge (think Amazon) and financed beyond normal local operations' abilities. That said, however, some make it work. It's a matter of aligning one's self with site developers who have the know-how to bring a page to the top of Google searches. Land on the top page or two and you've got a chance. It's called SEO, which is an acronym for search engine optimization. It's real, it's somewhat a science and the requirements change more frequently than those who work with it would like. Google often rewrites their algorithms in response to those who try to use their knowledge to "fool" the system. As with many other aspects of your business, your website and making it visible to the community is a job that is never truly completed.

Back to your brick and mortar store. Remember that proximity deals with location but also bear in mind that it deals with convenience as well. For example, if a customer were deciding where to go for a simple purchase, they would most likely think "close" first. But, if "close" meant heavy automobile traffic, long check-out lines, a parking lot that was difficult to get in and out of, rude employees, or higher prices, convenience might look different.

Look at that list again: heavy automobile traffic...can't control it; long check-out lines...can control it; parking lot difficult to get in and out of...somewhat controllable; rude employees... can be controlled; higher prices...somewhat controllable.

I want to make sure that you receive this key point: Proximity deals with both location and convenience. Location is pre-established (unless you're developing ground-up), but you can successfully offset some of negatives of a bad location by offering enough other advantages. Also notice that we jumped in and out of some of the other 6 Ps. Long check-out lines could be placed in People, parking lot might fall under Presentation, rude employees, People again, and higher prices, Price. So even though the discussion is of proximity, because proximity includes convenience, it would be incomplete without demonstrating how the 6 P's work together to influence buying decisions.

The category "People" is one of the six P's that is most easily controlled, but some managers don't do it very well. We have consulted with stores whose employees were rude, condescending or just not very knowledgeable. That's a really bad combination and I think you'd have to agree that any one of those attributes might make a store less appealing to its customers.

Here's something we've observed: attitudes start at the top, with the manager. I knew a guy who owned a store and managed it himself. Truthfully, he hated people—he knew it and his customers knew it. To his credit, and after a few years, he removed himself from day to day operations and placed someone in that position whose personality was less abrasive. The store improved, as you would expect. Attitudes of employees followed suit and soon the store was a much more pleasant place to be. Business increased and even the old grouch was pleased. I don't know how difficult it was for the new manager to run the gauntlet between the owner and the staff, but that's not the point here.

Operations are different. Some retail environments have a lot of interaction between customers and employees, others not so much. But there are always crucial "points of contacts". We'll help you sort those out and shore them up in Chapter 5.

Presentation is a P that is well within your ability to affect. Presentation deals with the way your store is "staged" within the theater within which it operates. Is it appealing, is it unique, and does it differentiate? We'll deal with a number of elements of presentation in weeks 1 and 2. We'll lift the blinders off your perception of your store's shopping environment.

The P that is promotion will be discussed in week 4. We often tell our customers that it's great to produce change, adapt knew try-harder principles, work to establish better pricing images etc. But unless you communicate those changes they go unnoticed for too long. The changes that you'll be undertaking represent a departure from your old business-as-usual. Past, present, and future customers need to know that. They might eventually learn from experience, or from word of mouth. But it will be more effective if you'll promote heavily, tell your story, and "toot your own horn". Tooting one's own horn is difficult for many people. In fact, it is one of the biggest challenges that my partner and I face in promoting our own business. But if not you, or not us, then who?

The discussion of pricing falls mostly in week 7, a little, perhaps in week 10. A friend and mentor once told me that pricing is not the main thing...it's the only thing. And although I disagreed with him then and would now, his message did spotlight how important it is to have a system, to work that system, and to establish a price image.

The last of the six P's is product, we'll deal with merchandising product in week 3, but that's not how products represent a differentiating factor for your store. When it comes to separating your store from others with products it becomes more questions like, does your store have unique products...products that are not readily available in close proximity? Or does your store have more depth or broader selections of products than other stores within your arena? If the answer to any one of these questions is yes, then product may be a differentiating factor for your store.

This book is not titled the 6 P's of differentiation nor is that its prevailing message. Whenever you discuss store changes, however, those changes need to be filtered through customers' eyes. Of course you'll always deal with the reality of financial restrictions and other issues that may affect your decisions.

Here's what I often suggest: Imagine a teeter-totter. If you put more weight on one end than the other, that ends falls to the ground. It must achieve near balance to hold both ends in the air. That is a good visual, I believe, for contemplating how your decisions affect both your bottom line (one end of the teeter-totter) and customers' perceptions of your store (the other end). One might conclude that a cash outlay to improve the shopping environment might send the bottom line crashing to the ground. The missing point is that by paying more attention to customers' perceptions of your store, by relationship, quite often enhances the bottom line. So what might have appeared to be wholly a cash outlay…simply an expense… effectively raises the other end of your teeter-totter at a near or even greater rate. Start actively viewing some expenses as investments and see how your perceptions change.

1. Don't Judge a Book by its Cover

It's an old cliché, isn't it? Don't judge a book by its cover may be good advice for some things, like people, perhaps. We shouldn't judge people by their appearances and I believe most would agree with that. But you get past people and back to other things, books, for example, like the cliché is talking about and, well, we all do it. It doesn't take a lot of brain matter to understand why that's important to your store. People make part of the decisions of where they will shop based upon how stores look from the outside. Your store's façade is, in essence, your book's cover.

Now before you disagree, if that was your intention, bear in mind that I'm not suggesting that the exterior of your store has to be beautiful, although it would be great if it was. I do believe however, that a store must be (1) seen and (2) changed occasionally and (3) look appealing and safe.

I am amazed how many store owners operate their stores for years, draw profits from them regularly and never reinvest in the cover. I know this to be fact, for many stores look the same outside as they looked 15 years ago. I've written a number of times about observing that store owners become blinded by seeing their stores day after day, week after week, month after month etc. It's almost as if the outside of their stores "disappear" to them. Nod you're head if you've noticed that too.

OK, here is the frightening part: Just as those stores disappear to their owners because of the same-old, same-old, they can also disappear to customers too. Not all of them, of course, but many people just stop seeing a store because it always looks the same. Please don't be one of those who cry out, "Well my customers know where I am and know what my store looks like...and they're fine with it". Don't be one of those.

Remember my D.O.A. (Dead on Apathy)? The life cycle of a store is such that operational deterioration is not overnight, but, rather, slower, yet sure if there has been no meaningful change. So the question becomes how can we open the eyes of the blinded?

For store owners themselves, sometimes it's as easy as focusing their attention. One of the things that we've found effective when we're consulting with customers is to take pictures of their buildings. Then we'll simply lay the pictures out before them and ask them what they see, or what they think. It's really quite entertaining to watch their faces and gauge their reactions. Sometimes the reactions are subtle, but often the images hit them like a ton of bricks and in a few extreme cases we noticed that store owners were actually ashamed of what they had failed to see. Those were the rare cases, but still, there were several of them.

One time my partner marched a store owner across the street from his business under the guise of buying him lunch. When they made it to the other side he simply turned around and looked at the customer's building without saying a word. As you would expect, after a few moments the store owner finally asked "what are you looking at?"

"Just wondering", Gary said.

"Wondering what?"

"I was wondering if you'd stop and shop this store, if you didn't own it."

Well as it turns out the customer got his free lunch, but I wonder if he also got a free case of indigestion. After all, his store's exterior was in bad need of a face-lift and he hadn't noticed it himself. When his focus was directed by another, he clearly saw what probably many of his customers had already seen. The store was ill-kempt, shoddy, dated, unappealing, and I could continue to add adjectives, they are adjectives, aren't they? But I won't.

Why would others see it, when he didn't? Let me explain it by dropping another old cliché on you... "He couldn't see the forest for the trees". His familiarity with the view had rendered him blinded to it.

How many customers had he lost because of it? That's impossible to guess and at the moment I don't remember how strong his competition was, but I do know the "cover of his book", his store's façade, was costing him business.

Happily, the story doesn't end there. When the manager confided that he didn't have the resources to spend on a new façade, Gary asked him if he could afford some paint. The store-owner shook his head sheepishly and that's the direction the story takes. He painted the building a rather bold color...a stark departure from the previous one. When Gary suggested the color he also recommended a source for flags to fly from the upper part of the façade and the results were amazing. Traffic increased, sales increased and the manager was thrilled.

I'm not sure that the new color made the building any more attractive...many might say that it didn't, but that's simply a guess. I do know, however, that the new color and the flags removed the store's "invisibility cloak"...at least for a time... and as they say the "proof was in the pudding". The manager told us stories of shoppers saying things like "I forgot you were here" or "are you a new business"?

Depending on your store and your situation, changing the color may not even be possible. I understand that. Some areas have strict covenants by which one must abide. Or, perhaps, your building has a brick façade and painting would be the last thing you would want to do anyway. Don't get caught up in the details and miss the bigger message. Focus on this: It will be a good use of your time and resources to explore ways that you might change-up your store's appearance.

Consider elements of your building you can change, can improve. For instance, in the case of the brick building, does it have awnings? If so are they fresh and vibrant or dull, faded, and unattractive? What would new colors do? A change of awnings and signs will often make a store look brand-spanking-new.

Remember the flags in the story above? Color, and particularly color in motion, attracts attention. Drive by a flea market or auto dealership where flags are waving in the breeze and you'll look, I know you will, you'll be unable not to. Do you think those flags are a good investment for the places that use them? I guarantee that they are.

How about banners? Consider banners. Banners can be large and colorful and they don't cost a lot. The trick with banners is to change them regularly.

I had a guy tell me one time that banners didn't work...so we went outside to look at the banner on the front of his building. He had one up which advertised a sale on something...I don't remember what. The banner was faded and had a small tear near one of the grommets.

"How long's that been up there?" I asked.

"Uh...I don't remember for sure...maybe 10 or 12 months...could be a little longer, I suppose."

"When you first put it up did people notice it?" I asked.

"Yeah, they asked about it for a while I think."

Folks, there was his problem. Remember the invisibility cloak? In this case, customers had seen his banner for so long that they no longer noticed it. Banners should not be used for long periods. Each one needs to be part of a program. When we sell a banner program it includes at least 6 banners. We instruct customers to rotate them every 4 weeks.

Make it easy on yourself...build a frame and use elastic ties or something similar so you can swap them out quickly and regularly. If you do, your messages will stay alive. I'm getting ahead of myself here though and we'll talk more about those kinds of things in week 4, the chapter on marketing and promotion.

OK, I don't want to do it, but I've got to. I don't want to talk to you about things as basic as weeds growing up in the seams of your parking lots and sidewalks, or trash near your entry way, or windows that look like they survived the dirty thirties...no I don't want to, but, I have to.

These things all fall under the "don't see the forest for the trees" discussion. In the grand scheme of your profitability, perhaps your knee-jerk reaction will be that these things don't matter. They do. They set the tone for what a customer expects from your store. In fact, I believe that if every other element of two stores was exactly the same but one manager paid attention to the details that I mentioned, his store would win. Shoppers' choices are sometimes based on large differences, but more often on the sum of the smaller ones. Be a smart manager, grasp this concept and begin to bring about changes.

How are you going to do it? We often work with store managers to write check lists to be used for follow up...next week, the week after that and beyond. With a checklist a manager can spend five minutes in analysis and be confident that he has covered the things that he's predetermined to be important.

Are the parking areas and sidewalks free of weeds? Check. Are the entry and vestibule areas trash free? Check. Windows clean and the signs hanging on them fresh, bright and accurate? Check. Shopping carts in place? Check. Building hosed down and free of dirt and dust? Check. You get the picture. It's not rocket science but you'd be amazed at what you'd encounter, if you had the opportunity to do what we do, and could see what we've seen.

One of my personal pet peeves is to see the back of displays when looking in through the front windows. If your store is small and such is unavoidable, we suggest using window film that communicates your branding message while hiding the eye-sores. Give us a call, if you like, and we'll help you out with this. There are always ways to address your store's individual characteristics.

Let's change gears. When you've finished reading this chapter, get in your car and drive by your store from both directions. How visible is it? We consulted with a store recently and took the manager on this type of discovery-drive for his store. From one direction the visibility might have rated 4 on a 10 scale, from the other it was even worse...maybe 1, 2 at the most. You just didn't see his store until you had nearly passed by.

This guy is a sharp individual and he didn't make the "well my customers know where I am" argument. I'm glad he didn't. That always reminds me of the old story of the farmer who was ticketed after failing to use his signal while turning into his own drive. "Everybody knows I live here" was his lame argument.

I love clichés. You've probably already picked up on that, but here's another one for you: "Out of sight, out of mind". Wow, that's a powerful message for store owners regarding their stores' visibility. I have mentioned the invisibility cloak that sometimes masks stores from customers. From one direction this store was almost *literally* invisible. It was a matter of how it sat in relationship to the frontage road and also to the lack of sufficient road-side signage. This is not a new store and it has been successful, but that's not the point. The question is how much more successful could it have been?

His answer was to address the roadside communication. He opted for an LED digital messaging board. He says that it has made a tremendous difference in traffic and in sales. No doubt the cash outlay will prove to be an excellent investment. In my opinion (and many others) these digital signs represent one of the most effective ways for stores to communicate, but we'll talk more about that in the chapter on marketing and promotion.

How's the parking at your store? Convenience in shopping is a big deal and accessible parking is a huge part of convenience. Many stores we've dealt with have had limited parking spaces. If that's the case with yours, analyze your space to see if there's another way of aligning cars that would give you more slots. Also, it should go without saying, but make sure your employees' cars are parked somewhere other than the premium spaces. While you're at it, check to see if the parking stripes are clearly visible as this is the way you communicate to customers how they should park. Finally, make sure the parking area is well-lighted if you maintain evening hours. Given recent events in virtually every part of our country, safety and vigilance have taken on higher levels of consciousness.

All of these suggestions have been small things. With the exception of the sign that I mentioned, the cost of all of them would be relatively low. If you've got a larger budget to work with, however, a new façade could give your store a real kick in the britches.

We were involved in a project in Western Kansas in which the store's outward appearance was changed as was the product mix and the interior layout. It's exciting to be a part of such renaissances. The new outward appearance was more attractive, but also was designed to complement the product offering. Simply by looking at the façade, and even without exterior signs, one might now guess that the building houses a home center. It now attracts new patrons and old ones who had, through the years, dropped away. The store is once again visible and now more attractive than ever.

We worked with another store located southeast of Dallas. We had designed for this gentleman before and so he called and asked us to take a look at another building he had recently purchased. He wanted us to give him ideas on how he might change and improve the façade without breaking the bank. The bigger investment, he knew, was coming with the major changes that the interior would require.

This was an easier project. The store had attractive lines, but had a lifted section at the entry that looked too big for the building's scale. We lowered it but maintained visual focus on the entry. We changed colors, added a bit of engineered stone, and voila: it turned out beautiful. It was not as simple as a paint job nor was it as complex as the completely redesigned facade. It was a wonderful and effective balance of solving challenges while minimizing expenses.

These are a couple of examples of how exteriors can be modified and updated. It is impossible to address specifics because every store is different. Receive this message: change is good.

That brings us full circle. Every element which can be viewed or otherwise interacts with customers from your store's exterior acts as the cover of your book. Competition begins not inside the store as many store owners would guess or suggest. Rather your store is vying for customers and dollars from the moment people pass by. So how about yours? How's your book's cover?

2. Interior Layout and Environment

With this chapter we're going to move inside. Let's start with the vestibule. Not all stores have a vestibule, but they would be better served if they did. A vestibule is a practical design because of its ability to buffer temperature changes between outside and inside. Because of this buffering effect the vestibule helps the operation to control utility costs.

For some reason the responsibility of vestibule maintenance often flies under the radar. It seems that whoever maintains the outside assumes that it's the responsibility of those who maintain the inside. Maybe those on the inside think that it's cleaned with the outside. Whatever the case, this is another "can't see the forest for the trees" alert. Many times we'll drive up to an attractive store only to find a mess in the vestibule. We take a few more steps; enter the interior, and, once again, the store looks pretty good.

Don't treat your vestibule as a storage facility for over stocked items. Don't use it to introduce new items or close-out old ones. Merchandise in the vestibule, in general, is a bad idea. For starters, there's no security out there. Merchandise displayed there might actually speed up on the evolutionary process, develop legs, and walk out on its own.

We consulted with a home center recently that decided it was a good idea to show a spattering of their rental products in the vestibule. They selected large items because, aware of security risks, they felt that these would be less likely stolen. They put signs up directing shoppers to their rental area to see an "even greater selection".

Dust and debris had blown in through the front doors and collected near the wheels of the equipment and in the now cluttered corners that were not readily accessible. Some pieces of the rental equipment were leaking drops of oil and even those that weren't smelled of gasoline. Long story short: The area was unattractive, smelled bad and started shoppers' trips off on the wrong feet. Keep your vestibule clean and relatively free of display. Was there a better way to communicate to shoppers about their rental products? Yes, and we'll cover that a little later.

If you've read many books or articles on retail operations you've probably heard or read that the impression a customer forms of your store happens within her first 10 steps into the environment. That is one of the reasons a store's "decompression zone" is so very important. A decompression zone is an area at the entry of a store, just inside of the vestibule, that is void of product and product-oriented displays. It can contain shopping carts, baskets or other items that might help shoppers with their shopping experiences. Its primary purpose is to allow shoppers to adjust to the new environment. Lighting, temperature, sounds, and smells are all different than the outsides'...the decompression zone acts to buffer the dramatic changes.

Decompression zone sizes will vary with store sizes. A small store will not have room for a 20' square decompression zone, but even when stores are small they will benefit from a properly scaled zone. Larger stores, on the other hand, will have more space available and often larger decompression zones make sense.

Beyond being space where shoppers can adjust to the changing environment, your decompression zone also sends signals regarding your store's size and the ease with which it will be shopped. It is, without fail, I believe, a good thing to make your store "feel" as large as it possibly can. Shoppers tend to characterize larger stores as having superior selections, better prices and more interesting environments.

A store with an open feel, upon entry, tends to feel more spacious overall. A store that has merchandise densely displayed in what should be an adjustment area can seem cluttered and small. Different people are more sensitive to a condensed environment than others. Put me in a store where clothing racks are arranged so that I am sweeping one as I shop another and I guarantee I won't be there long.

Research that has been done documents that I am not alone. This led to the coining of a new term. "Butt-brush" describes peoples' tendency to avoid shopping in areas in which they might inadvertently brush another person while shopping. This avoidance factor was even higher in women than in men and should be kept in mind not only in the front sections of the store but, really, all over.

A shopping trip to any store is an experience for its shoppers. Whether the experience is good or bad is subjective and will depend on many factors. But, a solid decompression zone is one of those factors so don't ignore it. Try to strip off your owner's or manager's hat as you evaluate yours.

Now, moving forward, as you walk past the decompression zone of your store what do you see? Scan from left to right and mentally take note of some key issues. Is the layout of your store such that it encourages browsing? A couple of points to look for: Make sure that your customer service counter is not in the main aisle and oriented ninety degrees from the aisle's traffic flow. If yours is, notice how it forms a natural barrier that seems to signal "stop" to a customer. Now, just the opposite point: if a customer is short on time can she readily see where she should go if she needs immediate assistance?

Try to evaluate as to whether the traffic pattern that you desire for your store is communicated through your fixture placement. What traffic pattern should you be trying to create? You want your store to be penetrated as deeply as possible. The sooner that happens the better off you are. Then even if a customer's shopping time is limited, he will still have to wind his way back through the heart of your products. It is for this reason that dairy products and meats most often reside at the back of a grocery store.

Let's take a look at your store's lighting. Is the lighting consistent and of sufficient brightness to make the environment look attractive, welcoming and safe? Are all of your light fixtures operational and free from that annoying, buzzing-ballast sound?

We compiled a lot of detailed information about lighting in Discovery-Based Retail. If you haven't read that book yet, I encourage you to do so. In this book I am dealing more with customers' overall perceptions of your store and how that might influence their store selection and their shopping behaviors. Therefore, take in your store's overall ambience and simply note whether the store looks dark or has dark sections.

It is very eye-opening to see how lumens can vary from area to area within the same store. The shopping pattern studies we have conducted during our research consistently show that a store's dark areas will not be as highly-trafficked nor will they produce commensurately to their brighter counterparts. Note what you have observed about your store's lighting and you can plan the way you will address the issues later. Now, it's time to change your focus.

Try to determine whether your store appears to be as big as it actually is. At first this may sound a little corny, but here's the reason I ask you to do this. Even small stores need to convey the feeling that they are open and spacious, thereby inviting exploration. Try to maximize site lines from the entry. Keeping the top line of your merchandise lower and consistent will help. Use bright murals on the farthest walls to encourage eyes to scan deeper into the store. Focused accent lighting at the end of your longest aisles is beneficial for the same reason. Make your notes and move on.

Now I want you to scan the communication elements in your store. Directive signs are important in promoting traffic distribution and increasing sales. Shoppers who readily find what they want will more likely make a purchase. Do you see department signs? How about categories within departments, are those marked? As you walk down your main aisles and scan to the left and then to the right do you see individual product location directories? If the answer to any of these questions is no, then you have identified opportunity to better guide your shoppers. If you act to correct these deficiencies the resulting increase sales should pay for the cost of the décor elements and this book many times over.

I once went through this exercise with a store's owner and the assessment of his communication pieces came up lacking. There were only a couple of departmental signs and nothing else. When I told him that he was missing the boat he began to tell me why signs weren't important in his store.

"Well, what you don't know," he said, "because I haven't told you is that we assist every customer that walks in our door. If they're looking for something, we make sure they find it."

I'm sure he believed what he said. But here's what I believe. If there was a clerk available for each and every customer each time one came in, there's simply too much staff. The cost of staffing one's store is one of the biggest items on a profit and loss statement. So in that case, signs to assist with customer service, if they allowed more judicious use of personnel would prove to be a wonderful investment.

A busy staff member could say "I'll be with you in a moment" while he was finishing with another customer or two, then directive signs could continue the customer on her shopping journey. It is true that we want customers to meander our stores; this will create additional impulse purchases. Customers who find themselves short on time will likely be irritated with a busy clerk in an environment where there are few or no guiding signs.

In addition, signs can also serve simply to make an environment more attractive. The colors and themes they add really do enhance a store's appearance. Now one last thing before we leave this subject. You may have a store in which a great deal was spent on décor...many years ago. Often a store owner recalls the investment, perceives the signs to still be adequate and quantifies their value based upon their original purchase price. Here's a news flash: they have paid you back many times. They're still functional, but they look dated, faded, and tired. They send messages to customers that your store is not progressive, perhaps it's even boring, and worst case scenario, struggling financially. Remember that the money it would take to modernize these important customer interface elements should be viewed as an investment and one that would add to the customer experience. Improve customer experience and you'll improve sales.

While you're still looking up, pay attention to the ceiling and whatever else is up there. It is beyond fathomable, and yet we see all the time, water-stained or even drooping or missing ceiling tiles. We see strings or wires left over from missing signs that were hung and removed years ago. We see heating units, duct work and ventilators just layered in dust. All of these things can be and should be corrected.

We recently completed a store plan for a gentleman who was gutting the existing building. His store had great ceiling height but the heaters and ducts which were all suspended in the space were distracting and looked very unappealing. We suggested he pick a color and darken the ceiling and those units. He was hesitant and heard from many people why they didn't think it would be a good idea. But he weighed the pros and cons and decided to do as we had suggested. He marked a line around the store and had the upper part, heaters, duct work and all, spray painted black.

During a recent phone call, he told me for the third time, at least, that he was super glad he had done it.

"It really makes the place shine", he said, "You don't pay any attention to those ugly units up there and for some reason it makes the store look even brighter and more appealing".

It's true, you don't and it did and it was a low-cost creative idea to "upscale" the look of his environment. Have you ever noticed in many galleries how the darkened ceiling adds so much interest to what is below? It's because, I believe, whatever is below becomes your total focus.

Let's walk your store now. There are a number of things I want you to watch for as we do. Depending on product offering and the types of displays you have, you'll have to modify this to your own operation, but I'm sure you'll have no problem doing that.

Walk down each aisle making sure that shopping carts can easily pass. Are the aisles free of clutter and merchandise? I don't mind seeing a stack of shopping baskets or perhaps a nice floor stand display at the aisle's end, but that's it. I don't want to see boxes cut open, and left for any purpose. I don't want to see two-wheelers unless they're being used at the moment. I don't want to see litter in the aisles. Also make sure that there are no items that protrude beyond the base decks and shelves. These can actually be safety hazards.

We once walked the floor with the owner of a home center. He was appalled when we pointed out that there were metal flanges displayed and protruding beyond a gondola's base deck. The flanges themselves, which were thin metal, could have easily sliced a customer's leg as they passed by. He realized the liability ramifications and corrected the problem immediately.

Just as a change of pace, if yours is a ready-to-wear boutique, make sure there are not articles of clothing on the floor around your racks...we see it all the time and it really does downgrade the look of the rest of the merchandise.

Now focus on the fixtures themselves. Are all of the fixtures' components in place? Check the top caps, the toe kicks, and the side trims. Missing pieces are small things that focus attention away from your merchandise. You don't want your customers' attention to be distracted from your products for any reason.

As you glance down side counters which have peg-boarded items, notice if the hooks are of the same length. If they are, the counter will look nice and uniform, neat and appealing. If they're not, you'll notice that it gives the presentation a less than ideal look.

We'll speak about merchandising in the next chapter. For now, go compile and organize your notes. What you should be shooting for from these exercises are A-Z task lists for your employees.

3. Merchandising and Other Stuff

Merchandising is fun to talk about and, for me it's fun to write about too. It is both art and science, and contributes greatly to a store's sales. Although you may find it surprising, it also has a lot to do with a store's margin too. Therefore I identify it as one of the key elements to your store's success.

Merchandising rules vary with stores' offerings. I'll be discussing merchandising hard goods but many of the points I make, you will find educational for soft lines too. Let's go back out to your sales floor and take a look around.

The first things I want you to notice are your end caps. End caps are kind of a mystery in most small singularly owned stores...in large chains, not so much. If you go into a Wal-Mart, or Target, or Lowes or ...you fill in the name, you'll see end caps merchandized correctly. They adhere to some of the same guidelines I was taught 30 or more years ago during my management training with the T.G. & Y. stores company.

Back then I was taught that an end cap looks and performs best with a single-product featured on the display. In rare cases a couple or three products could be combined for a theme, but the down side was, if the products all had different prices, which often they did, the display was difficult to sign effectively.

End caps are considered premier space in retail stores and when you see the way they are utilized in the large stores that I mentioned, it's easy to understand why. In those environments the end caps are bulked up with merchandise which is attractively priced, signed to garner attention and then changed frequently. These end caps "sales machines" obviously produce great amounts of profit.

If you read the introduction to this book, you read about chain stores being directed or controlled by what we call a "giant thinking head". The "giant thinking head", of course, is just a visual key I use to describe all of the systems that are in place in this type of corporate environment. It is not meant to be derogatory. It simply implies that the corporate systems give their stores tremendous advantages.

The successes these stores have with their end cap programs, for example, are highly dependent upon the processes. First of all, corporate buyers make large purchases. They send large amounts of the end cap items they bought to the individual stores, send pictures or plan-o-grams of how the displays should look. They assign dates as to when the end caps should be displayed and then top it off by suggesting prices that have been preordained by corporate price shoppers. That's all nice, neat and tidy, isn't it?

The only problem is that if you're not the beneficiary of a "giant thinking head" you have to replicate the process, best you can, on your own. How you doing with that? Well, that's why we're out here on the sales floor looking around again. Do you see some end caps that are no longer features (if they once were) and are now, instead, simply 36" of merchandise that didn't fit on a side counter?

Evaluate how many end caps you're *effectively* using for promotional items. It's going to sound weird to you, but the ones that are left, the ones you're using for side-counter over flow items, knock them down and get them off the floor. You'll find that the side counters down those aisles are more open and inviting. You'll also learn that the orphan items that you'll be moving back to side counters are easier for customers to find when they're where they should be. It's a matter of adjacency...items being where customers expect them to be.

Develop a program for the end caps that you've chosen to leave as promotional features. The program needs to be thought out well in advance, a year-long program is great. Use a floor plan drawing to number each end cap. Identify items that would be timely for the various seasons and then make plans to buy those items. It makes sense to buy them during promotional periods, doesn't it? Vendor markets are a great time to take advantage of deals. The other advantage is that once your promotional period is over, and the items return to the regular prices, you'll be able to realize a few extra margin points. The most important part of the whole process is the process itself.

Detail your plan to include dates at which the items will be switched out. Identify what items will be on what end caps, schedule buying those items and then make sure that the merchandise has arrived by the time your promotion is supposed to start. Price-shop your competitors' stores on the items that will be featured and get in the "ball park". I don't really want to encourage you to try to beat your competitors, at least not the big box ones. That is a fight that is difficult to win. Still your price should be competitive. Become a stickler for details and demand adherence to your new program. Put someone in charge of the mechanics. Make sure that they fully comprehend how important this program is to the store team's success.

I would encourage you to change the merchandise out at least every other month. In an ideal world it would be more frequent, but I am aware of the constraints you face. As part of your master plan you can just relocate end caps from one part of the store to another. This gives a new look to the environment and shoppers something different to see. I was always amazed, as perhaps you have been too, that an item that didn't sell in one location was a "lights-out" success at another. Even this rotation process, if you choose to make it part of the plan, write into your program. Document it, refine it and repeat it.

One last thought; if you choose to feature items you normally carry, you'll have a built-in system for liquidating the merchandise once your promotional period is over. If you choose new items, items you don't normally stock, you'll add interest to your store. Shoppers will be surprised and that's good. It keeps a store exciting for its customers. It does demand, however, that you "pre-think" what you'll do with the merchandise that doesn't sell. Regular markdowns will work to purge the stuff, but they will also adversely affect your margins so keep that in mind. It becomes a matter of balance, I believe. Some end caps featuring new items and some featuring more value on everyday items might be the perfect blend.

OK, you've developed the system, the merchandise has arrived, now let's talk about merchandising it. If you haven't already, you'll have to teach your employees what you expect from them. End caps are a great place to start teaching merchandising.

We're going to assume that all of the items are the same size. Remember we decided to buy one item per feature end cap. First determine whether you'll be using shelves or peg hooks. Now begin at the bottom of the display, place an item on the base deck to check it for height. Instead of loading up the base deck however, leave the single item there. Place your first shelf just above the item you placed on the deck. Adjust the shelf so that there is not much space between it and the top of the item...just enough for a shopper to easily pull the item from the display. Now place one of the items on that shelf, don't load it either but, instead, repeat the process. You'll do this until you get to the top of the end cap. The reason you don't load the shelves as you go up is because you don't yet know where your display will end in relationship to the top. If you get up there and have an awkward 8" empty space, move back to the first shelf and adjust each one proportionally to ensure the featured items end just below the product sign.

Once you have adjusted your shelves to bring your items to near the top, you can go back and load them. You don't want a lot of space between shelves and here's the reason. By "facing" product, and by that I mean pulling items to the front of the display, you can make a display look fuller than it may actually be. The closely-placed shelves will hide shoppers' downward views. If there is empty space behind a row or two of product it won't be seen. You want your customers to think you bought a ton of the item, thereby getting a great price which you are now passing on. Creating the illusion that your shelves are full may not be important when you first set up the feature for they may actually be loaded. But, hopefully, it will become important as the product starts to sell down later in the promotion. One last point, before you ever walk away from your new display, double-check that your feature price has been placed.

Let's look at the side counters now. Each department within your store will have categories. Each category will have product groupings. Let me give you an example from the hardware industry. Hardware stores traditionally have a tool department. Within that department there are two divisions; hand tools and power tools. Let's just focus on hand tools. Within hand tools there are many categories, striking tools, for instance, is one of those categories.

But as we drill down even further (no pun intended) within striking tools we'll realize that it becomes segmented into smaller groups; claw hammers, rip hammers, ball peen hammers, engineers hammers, sledge hammers, tack hammers, rubber mallets and on and on. This type of departmental and categorical divisions and sub-divisions are present in nearly every product offering out there.

One of the first things to realize is that we want to make the shopping task easier. We want shoppers to find the department, sub-department, category and sub-categories that they want, quickly. That was the main reason for all of the guiding signs that we discussed earlier, wasn't it?

Now we must ensure that products are separated in a fashion that makes sense to the shopper. In our example of hammer types, for instance, we don't want a tack hammer, merchandized with engineer hammers or a sledge hammer in the middle of the claw hammers. The more sense your display makes to your shoppers the more likely they are to find exactly what they want. If they do so with ease they'll develop better opinions of your store.

Let's say that we have now separated our striking tools into their various sub-categories and are ready to merchandize. For this example we'll say that we have 8' of gondola space. Also, just so we're on the same page, let's say that the island gondolas are 6' high.

Let's focus on 4' of space at a time because the uprights of the gondolas make natural divisions in side counters and if shelves become necessary, the divisions will look uniform.

OK, stand in front of the empty gondola section. Imagine that emblazoned on our 4' wide by 6' high section of gondola is a cross...a cross like Jesus was hung from. The cross's height is 6' and its span is 4'...just the size of the gondola.

That makes a great visual image for illustration. Now, if you imagine a horizontal band running parallel from 12" above the crosses arms to 12" below, you'll be visualizing what will be the "high-performance" area of this gondola. The right side of the horizontal strip will likely even out-perform the left.

10 Weeks to a Better Retail Operation

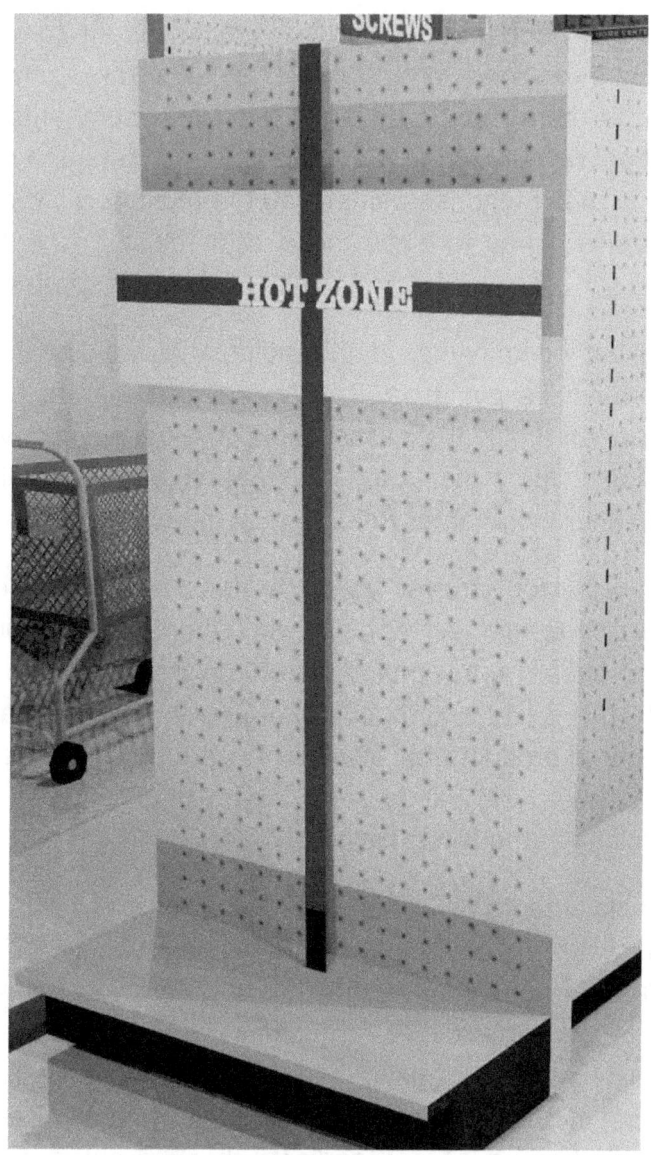

So what? How does knowing this help you?

Within every sub-product category you'll have an item that, given the choice, you'd rather sell. It's the item that produces more margin dollars. So as you merchandise, it would be a great idea to run a report and understand which items in the categories benefit you the most. It will then be a matter of trying to place those items closest to this hot zone.

You might be thinking, at this point, that we have some inconsistencies going on. If we're not to separate a sub-category isn't it likely that the whole strip becomes devoted to a single type of item? It could happen, but it's not likely, if you adhere to another rule...vertical merchandising.

There was, for several years, a debate about whether product performed better displayed in horizontal ribbons or vertical ones. I think that there's little dispute any longer and to me it just seems common sense. If I were take a category of product that of which I need 12 square feet to merchandize, I could do so in several fashions but let's take a look at the two extremes.

If I display the items in a narrow horizontal band, since my display will take 12 square feet, it would measure 12' long and 1' tall when I was finished. So now my shoppers would have to pace back and forth in order to see the entire offering. They would likely miss some products because, standing in one place, they wouldn't see them all. Keeping in mind what we learned earlier, either the entire offering would span 3 different sections' hot spots or, if displayed above or below the high-performance zone, none of it.

Now visualize the same 12 square feet of merchandise displayed vertically. Because the gondola is 6' high it would require a 2' band from top to bottom. Displayed this way, we'd have part of the sub-category's product crossing the high-performance area and the other parts above and below. A person could stand in one spot and by simply moving their eyes up and down, easily scan the entire display. Now armed with your new found knowledge, you would have the ability to increase your margin in this category.

You would determine which items of the sub-category would benefit you most when they sold (these will likely be the highest margin items) and you would place those items in the high-performance band. The items that must be extremely competitively priced and, therefore, produce lower margins, you would move to the display's base. It won't stop the sale of the promotional items, but it will increase the likelihood that shoppers buy the higher margin items more frequently.

It's interesting to go into a store which operates under a "giant thinking head" and see this in action. For example during a recent shopping trip to Wal-Mart, looking for ink pens, I found the high-profit zone of the pen section completely filled with pens that were packaged either one or two per sleeve. These pens were higher in price, probably higher quality, and looked very appealing.

But I was looking for some pens to use for an upcoming presentation. They needn't be high quality because I was going to give them away and I would likely see them left lying on tables once the presentation was completed.

Guess where I found my low-priced pens? Yep, you're right. They were on the base deck. No doubt, the "giant thinking head" had determined that Wal-Mart would be better served by selling the single and double packed pens which would obviously produce higher margins. It is also important and educational to note that the higher margin pens were the ones that were flagged with "shelf talkers". Shelf talkers are the little signs put in place to draw customers' attention to where the merchant will benefit most.

There are other considerations when merchandising side counters...some which will affect margin and others that are simply mechanics. In the latter group, for example you'll want to try to keep the larger items lower in the display. Visualize a pyramid, big at the base and smaller at the top. That's a good image to merchandize by. At this point you may be wondering how you can do both if, for instance, a larger item is also one of your best margin items? After all, it can't go low in the display and in the high-performance zone at the same time, can it?

You'll have to use your judgment and of course there will be exceptions to all guidelines when it comes to merchandizing. For me though, I would adhere to the margin-increasing rule if possible. I'm buttering my own bread first, if you get my drift.

Here's a point that deals with both margin and mechanics. The question inevitably arises: should I merchandize products by size, large to small or small to large? You'll see it done both ways, but studies have shown that most people will reach for the item on the right. So, as another general rule merchandize your larger sizes of the same products to the right. This action, over time and after many customers, should incrementally increase your sales.

Allow me to mention a few more matters of mechanics. We discussed breaking your side counter into 4' increments for the topic of hot spots, but now let's take a look at the full length of the counter and note things you should be watching for.

Assure that your peg board hook lengths are all the same on a side counter. They can vary from counter to counter, but as a customer scans the length of an individual gondola the hooks should be uniform. The uniform appearance will make the overall presentation more attractive and, therefore, more appealing to customers. Also, if you are using shelves, the gondola looks more attractive if the shelves are running the same height from section to section. Obviously this is not always possible because of varying sizes of products, but my point is this: if you can adjust a shelf a notch one way or the other to keep it in line with the adjacent section, do so. You'll find this simple procedure improves the looks of the display too.

Are you familiar with the term cross-merchandising? It refers to the placement of same product in more than one location in your store. It makes a lot of sense and especially for those products that a customer might expect to find in more than one place. A great example of one such product from the hardware industry is duct tape.

If ever a more versatile product was invented I'm not aware of it. Duct tape can easily be merchandised in the paint section, the hardware section, the electrical area, lawn and garden...and so on. There may be as many places to merchandize duct tapes as there were ways in which Bubba Gump could cook shrimp. When unsuspecting customers come in contact with one of your strategically placed impulse displays of duct tape your register will ring merrily.

There is no need to devote a permanent home in each department for this type of impulse cross-merchandising, but rather, use one of a number of different types of clip strips or other impulse merchandising devices. Keep in mind that it makes sense to select high-margin items for impulse cross-merchandizing.

I guess this week's discussion wouldn't be complete without addressing customer check-out areas and how you can benefit from strategically placed impulse displays there. In some stores, shoppers line up and wait for the "next available team member". While they are marching in line, shoppers walk a gauntlet area which displays high-margin treats and gadgets. I have been victimized by this strategy in one of my favorite stores many times. It is a store that specializes in all things having to do with computers and technology. I know full well that I'll be herded through a 30' line which is loaded with goodies on both sides...flash drives, key chains, candy bars, phone cases…the list goes on and on. Here's the kicker. I know it's there, I know its purpose and yet I still love it. It makes the time waiting for a checker pass quickly. For this reason some of our most recent store designs have incorporated this device.

4. Marketing, Branding, and Reaching Out

I have had the awesome privilege to address several organizations on the topics of branding, marketing and advertising. I believe that although people understand, in broad concepts, the three topics, they really seem to benefit from focusing on the subjects individually and then collectively. As you read this chapter, please take notes as to how the information pertains to your specific operation.

Let's start with brand. My first recollection of the word "brand" had nothing to do with retail at all. In fact, my first many-years-long exposure to the word couldn't have been further from our retail subject.

Having grown up on the farm, I knew from an early age that it was common practice for cattle to be branded. Cowboys would first round up their cattle and build large bon-fires. They then placed "branding-irons", which were long thin handles affixed with a symbol that represented whatever ranch they were branding for, into a fire. Rocking R and Lazy S are two brands that come to mind. Those were probably symbols that were used on more than one episode of Bonanza or Gun Smoke. I'm dating myself aren't I? Once the rancher's iron symbol was glowing red-hot, one by one, the cattle were wrestled to the ground and the pattern burned into their hide. From that point forward the animal had a symbol of ownership affixed to it. It was a distinct point of differentiation. Keep that in mind; we'll come back to it. I first want to tell you about my other early recollection of the word "brand".

You'll probably think I watched too much television as a kid, and you'd probably be right. One show that I always liked was a show called "Branded". It starred a guy named Chuck Connors who also played as The Rifleman in another popular television series of the time. The set-up for the show was interesting and also gives us great clues into something you should understand about the branding of your store.

Each week as the show began, the set-up played again. Connor's character had led a division of troops into a battle years earlier...I don't recall the details. But, somehow in the smoke and intensity of the fight and although he had been fighting valiantly, he became separated from the rest of his men. The story line revealed that the rest of his troop had been killed during that separation and he was the only remaining survivor.

Each week the series began by showing Connors standing at attention while his superior officer stripped the rank insignias from his shoulders, tore his buttons from his dress uniform, pulled his sword from the scabbard at his side, broke it in half, and tossed the pieces out through the fort's compound doors. It was unimaginable shame for the lead character who had been wrongly accused. From that point on, and through the end of the series Connor's character was forever:

>"Branded, marked as the one who ran."

"What do you do when you're branded?"

"But you know you're a man."

Even though he was innocent of the accusations, deserter was a "brand" that followed him everywhere.

But what do all these cowboy shows have to do with your store? What can we learn from this nonsense? Well, let's see.

Everything you'll read in trade magazines and books will tell you that it is important that you build your store's brand. I agree completely. But what is it? You have to know what it is before you can work at building it, don't you? I'm going to use the stories I just relayed to help formulate a working definition for store brand. My hope is that as you understand it better, you can work at improving yours.

First, just like cattle are branded to show ownership and differentiation, so too does your store's brand differentiate it. In the case of the cattle brand, it was a single character...a symbol affixed to the rump. I don't think you want to go there. But if you'll start thinking about every which way that you can differentiate your store, make it stand out, and separate it from the herd, then you're on your way to understanding store brand.

Here's something I don't want to forget to mention: I have asked people what the McDonalds Restaurant brand is. Sometimes they'll answer, it's the golden arches. It was trick question, of course. The golden arches are the logo for McDonalds just like the blue oval is the logo for Ford.

Neither symbol is a brand. It's likely that you've got a logo for your store too. You may also have a buzz-phrase that appears with your advertisements. Think Southwest Airlines "Lowest fare in the air". Both logos and branding phrases are parts of a brand...but they're not the entirety of the brand.

If we end our quest for a definition of the word "brand" at this point, I guess it would be something like "all things by which your store is identified". That would work pretty well, because it would include the logo and branding phrases we just discussed. It would also include things like your store's customer service. Provided, that is, that customer service were something you had worked on hard enough that customers would immediately associate great customer service with your store. Gosh it would even include the bright yellow color you painted the exterior to stand out from the crowd. But, wait there's something missing, I'm afraid.

Remember the frontier soldier standing at attention while he was humiliated in front of his fellow soldiers? I mentioned that that scene set the tone for each of the subsequent episodes. The soldier went around doing good, best he could, but because of the cloud that hovered over him...his "brand", he was treated disrespectfully by most of the people he ran in to.

So now, let's bring this full circle and complete our definition of brand as it applies to your store.

Brand is all things by which your store is identified, both good and BAD.

So if you've worked hard to establish the fact that your store is competitively priced, that's _possibly_ part of your brand. If you've worked hard to never be out of stock on items your customers expect you to have, that's _possibly_ part of your store's brand. If your store is thought of as having convenient hours, that's _possibly_ part of your store's brand. The list, obviously, could go on from here, but hopefully, by this point the underscore and italics have spiked your attention.

The reason there is a "possibly" in front of each of these characteristics is to draw your attention to the fact that the opinions must be those of customers and would-be customers, not yours or your staffs'.

You may believe that you are competitively priced, for example. But if we surveyed 100 customers, or "would-be-could-be" customers, would 80% of them perceive that to be true and agree with you? By the way, there is no magic about the 80%. It's just important to understand that all of branding is ultimately graded by consumers so it would need to be a good percentage of the "possibilities".

I made the statement early in this chapter that by fully understanding brand you would be able to work toward improving yours. If you ever saw the movie "Forest Gump", you might remember a scene in which Forest (Tom Hanks) was running, and had been, for days for--"no particular reason".

As he ran along he was joined by others. During this particular scene an unshaven runner sped up to run beside Hanks and, then, said something like, "Oh, man, you just stepped in dog shit."

Forest looked down calmly as he ran and responded flat pan, "It happens."

His running-mate then asked "What does…shit does?"

To which Forest replied "Sometimes".

Of course, in a follow up scene we are led to believe that the "Shit happens" t-shirts that were worn only a few years earlier had been the result of this chance encounter.

I believe this: Shit may happen sometimes, but brand will happen every time. Your store will have a brand…it will have "things by which it is identified, both good and bad". The advantage of completely understanding your store's brand is that it will allow you to actively "steer" it, rather than simply letting it happen.

Steering your brand should begin by brainstorming about what you want it to be. Part of this process should include understanding how your store is slotted within the arena within which it competes. I'm not going to cover "store slotting" in this book. Please refer to Chapter 8, "A Slot for Success", in Discovery-Based Retail.

But after understanding how your store is slotted you'll have a better list of achievable possibilities for branding characteristics. Let' say, for example, that your store is slotted as a regional competitor within your trade territory. One of the characteristics of a regional-competitor type slotted store is that it must be priced competitively. Therefore you determine that you want your store to be known for (branded) as competitively priced.

Your plan for marketing a competitive price image as a branding message might go something like this:

- Perform extensive competitive price shops.
- Identify areas where you are the most competitively priced.
- Identify areas where you need to work to lower pricing.
- Develop a pricing structure that will moderate the worst "highs" without negatively impacting your overall gross margin.
- Place "Our Low Price" or similar flags on products which you have lowered or that you have determined will make your best price presentation.
- Consistently include this message in all of your marketing communications.

You'll notice we started with the research instead of the message. If you're going to advertise that you have competitive prices, then it should be so. If you started advertising without the supporting data, it's not a message that either you or your staff could buy into, get behind, and sell. You wouldn't know for sure it if were true. The only way to get that information and then make sense of it is through lots of leg and brain work. But it's worth it. *You want your marketing messages to ring with truth and sincerity.*

Perhaps I lost some of you on the price image thing. Maybe some are thinking...I can't be priced that competitively and still maintain the margin that it takes to keep my business viable.

If that's you and those are your thoughts, here are a few different things to think about. The first likelihood is that your store is not slotted as a regional competitor at all, but rather as a *convenience* or *product-driven niche* store. Once again, if those two terms aren't familiar please check out the book [Discovery-Based Retail](#) on Amazon. You'll learn that if your store is slotted as a convenience or product-driven niche type store pricing is several layers down on what attracts people to your operation.

If you still believe that you are a regional competitor, however, but find that you're having difficulty competing while maintaining a viable margin, it becomes a question of determining if your current margin is comparable to your industry. If it is and you're still struggling with profitability you'll need to examine expense control...if it isn't you need to determine if you're using the proper suppliers and buying right.

We'll talk more about pricing and expense control later. Let's get back to steering your brand. If price image is not a branding characteristic that you choose to use, pick out others. It's not important to have a large number of branding theme characteristics. In fact it will probably work better if you choose 2 or 3 and really hammer those messages home.

- "The most conveniently located "your-store-type" in the valley.
- Store hours that stretch your day.
- We offer expert assistance in every department.
- Free in-store interior decorators always available.
- Free same-day delivery.
- Certified Kitchen designers on staff.
- No-hassle return policy.
- Finest quality—always!

You get the message. It is important to (1) conceptualize fact-based branding messages and (2) Communicate the messages over and over and over.

Now that you fully understand brand, let's discuss how you will communicate it. Within your tool box of communication you have three devices: 1. Marketing 2. Advertising and 3. Interpersonal communication.

I guess the first question is a simple one. Are marketing and advertising the same thing? The answer is no. Marketing is the bigger animal...if that makes sense...if not, hopefully it soon will.

First let's look at an accepted definition of marketing.

The American Marketing Association (AMA) states, *"Marketing is an organizational function and a set of processes for creating, communicating and delivering value* to customers and for managing customer relationships in ways that benefit the organization."

That definition might work for some people, but within the context of this book and this discussion, it just seems too ambiguous and fuzzy around the edges for me. Given our new understanding of what brand is, it seems that we need a more succinct, understandable and actionable definition.

- *Marketing is the process of communicating and steering your brand.*

It's simple and understandable. Immediately you know that the branding messages that you've developed are what your communications will center around.

But wait a minute. While we're getting our definitions out of the way let's tackle the term advertising. Remember I said that advertising and marketing are two different things so here you go:

- *Advertising is a form of communication that <u>persuades</u> people <u>to purchase</u> a product or service.*

In seminars we've had people joke that if that is truly the definition of advertising then perhaps they've never advertised at all because it seems they hadn't persuaded many people to buy. All joking aside there are some guidelines to making your advertisements more effective and we'll cover those in a moment.

Before we do there are some thoughts that need to be finished. I mentioned that you have 3 tools in your communication tool box: Marketing, Advertising and Personal Communication.

Personal communication involves the traditional aspect of sales associates interacting with customers. This is very important and we'll deal with the subject in more detail later. But the point that I want to make here is that the Personal Communication tool is changing.

Social media has brought together communities that literally include people from across the street, across the country and around the world. It seems that some savvy retailers have been able to leverage Facebook and Twitter to this end. I want to acknowledge it and how it fits into brand communication today. I am no expert on the social mediums however and will not write about them extensively. Suffice it to say that as you are computing your store's communication budget, depending on your store type and audience, you may need to give attention to this exploding phenomenon.

You can see at this point that marketing and advertising overlap. For example any advertisement could contain marketing messages. Something that was strictly a marketing piece, however, would probably not contain prices because its primary function is to communicate branding messages.

If you look for a quantifiable R.O.I. (return on investment) on marketing pieces you won't find it. Although you hope to move your store to higher levels of awareness in peoples' minds the purpose of marketing pieces is not to "persuade people to purchase". Pieces which would do that would fall under advertising.

This begs the question then: Should you expect an R.O.I. on your advertising pieces. Yes...and no. I say this because of a couple of key points. You'll hear these points hammered over and over by those who sell all kinds of advertising: Frequency and repetition.

Frequency refers to how often your messages are communicated over a specific time span. Repetition refers to how often that time period is repeated. Although stressing that repetition and frequency are important may come across as sales-speak from an advertising salesperson, keep in mind that I have no horse in the race. It is merely an observation I have made over the years.

So back to the question should you expect an R.O.I. on your advertising? Remember I stated earlier, yes and no. Yes, on R.O.I. for your entire advertising program, no, not necessarily on individual campaigns.

We consult with many locations on a monthly basis using a budgeting system we have developed that we call The Profit Explorer. We have the opportunity to work with varying types of locations and operations with this program, see their monthly results, and draw conclusions. We have observed that there is often a very dramatic correlation between moneys spent on advertising during a specific month and the results of that month.

Let's say for example that a store had an advertising piece circulated that had 20 items on it. A store manager might track the sales of those 20 pieces during the promotion, note that their margins had suffered because of the campaign, do simple arithmetic and conclude that he had not received an R.O.I. on the cash expenditure.

When the week of the campaign is more closely viewed in retrospect, however, and the total sales and margin dollars that were produced during the promotion are computed, the owner finds an increase in volume and margin coming from other items throughout the store. One could not be certain that the entire "bump" came as a result of the promotional piece. But, providing the retailer did the job of educating employees to "sell up" and the store was merchandised with adjacencies that promoted related products' features and benefits, it would be likely that there was a direct correlation.

Let's discuss for a few moments characteristics that make an advertising piece more effective. Good advertising pieces should include:

1. An interrupter.
2. An engagement.
3. An informational exchange.
4. Direction for proceeding to the desired conclusion.

An interrupter is just what it sounds to be. An interrupter diverts peoples' attention from their surroundings, from their reverie, or from competitive ads. I can be watching a television show, for example, and be completely disengaged during commercials. Unless the advertisement does something to amuse me, startle me or entertain me, I will likely fade into disinterest. I need to be interrupted from my current state.

Similarly, if I find a fist full of advertising pieces in my mail box, a piece must grab me by separating itself from everything else that has been delivered. In this case the interrupter might come in the form of an image, an eye-catching color or a creative headline.

Once an advertising piece has interrupted a viewer, reader or listener, a well structured transition must follow. We'll refer to this as the "engagement". The engagement must segue from the interrupter, transforming it into something that I, the customer, will perceive as beneficial or desirable.

If that step is successfully completed an informational exchange often follows. Within or during the informational exchange an item's features will be translated into customer benefits making it increasingly likely that the reader/viewer will take the final step.

The final step is often instruction from the advertised item to "buy me" …but not always. A low risk way in which a next step can be taken is often a better strategy.

Allow me to explain this using an advertisement example outside of retail to clearly illustrate the principles. Let's say that an orthodontist want to advertise his service for applying corrective braces.

He might choose as an interrupter a picture of a person who has terrifically crooked teeth. Just to heighten the impact he might also choose the picture in which the crooked teeth clearly demonstrate that they are difficult to clean and maintain. This might all be done against a bright red background. The overall presentation would definitely interrupt.

The point of engagement might be something as short and simple as "Are you comfortable with your teeth?" Of course, those who were, would disengage at this point, but remember they wouldn't have been targets anyway...we captured their interest only by virtue of the strength of our interrupter.

We have engaged the attention of our targets now. It is time to move to the informational exchange portion of the communication piece. It might include features like: improved bite, improved smiles, and improved hygiene. The features might be translated into these corresponding benefits: better digestion, higher degrees of self-confidence, more attractiveness and better overall health.

At this point, it is time for us to direct our reader or viewer to action. Often the action is just the display of a very competitive price that subliminally says "buy me" to the audience. But in the case of our orthodontics ad the better direction might be to "call for your FREE consultation". We are not asking the customer to spend money, only to take the next step.

Early in my career I would often run cabinet sales at the small lumber yard that I managed. I opted for an advertisement that showed discount percentage off list prices. That type of number is difficult for a customer to quantify but the attractive kitchens in the communication pieces really did attract attention.

My desire was not to sell cabinets directly from the ad or even in the store, really. Instead, I would push for an opportunity to meet with prospects in their homes. I found that the sales I completed on "their turf" were usually much larger than what I could sell in our store. If we would have had a state of the art showroom like you see in some home centers today, I don't know if the same would have held true. But I suspect it still would have. I had the opportunity to view their situations and challenges and invariably it seems that this process generated stronger relationships. So the call to action in my cabinet ads was "free in-home no-obligation estimates".

It may be difficult to identify these four steps in every advertisement that you'll see, but often they will be clearly delineated.

You have now learned how to properly structure your advertisement pieces. Where should you invest your advertising dollars? This is a question that will have no one-answer-fits-all, but there are points and strategies worthy of discussion.

First and foremost it is more important than ever to have a strong web presence. If you don't have a website, get one. If you have a website that was built years ago and looks the same as it did back then, you don't have a website. If you don't have a website that is constantly growing, you don't have a website.

There are resources that allow customers to build and host websites for very little cost. The problem is that once you're done you really don't have much. The site will most likely not be S.E.O. friendly, which means that you won't get many of the surfers out there who are looking for your products or services.

S.E.O. is an acronym for "search engine optimization". Content for a website must be structured to produce the desired results. Keywords and key phrases must appear at tactical positions within content to ensure search engine visibility. Content which has been authored in this fashion is one of the elements computed within the algorithms that search engines like Google, for example, use to determine who will appear on the first page, second page, etc of a search.

If your site appears on the 12th or the 112th page of a search it is unlikely it will be viewed by surfers. Other elements that affect search engine placement are things like the age of a site. A mature site, providing it is dynamic and growing, will achieve better results than a new site. If the site is old and has had no changes forever, it will end up lower in the pile.

A site that has 100 pages of worthwhile content will typically score higher in a search than a smaller one. It makes sense, then, for the site to continually expand. As a site expands it does get more difficult to maintain, but that should be the job of your specialist.

Also the number of "inbound" and "outbound" links a site has will affect its ranking too. I should let you know that the quality of inbound links is also a determining factor...in other words, are the sites that are linking to yours fairly heavily trafficked? A link to a junk site will have no impact.

As an example of what S.E.O. can do for a site here are some of the search terms we have targeted for our site discoverdbr.com and where each ranks on Google.

- Hardware store layout   First page
- Hardware store design   First Page
- Store layout   First Page
- Retail store lighting tips   First Page
- Visual merchandising tips   First Page
- Retail atmospherics   First Page
- Grocery store layout   First Page

None of these rankings have been purchased through pay-per-click (bought). As of this writing, we do not purchase site traffic. The rankings have been generated through a lot of work and perseverance. I show you this not to be a "look how good we are" thing, but rather to demonstrate that traffic can be generated organically and that that should be your goal.

Here's a simple practical consideration for your site; remember to have your telephone number appear on the browser's tab and prominently on each site page. Desk top surfers, mobile and pad internet users alike, have replaced their yellow pages with browsers. Make sure all of your contact information is easy to find.

One of the strategies some businesses are using successfully is email marketing. We build and maintain sites for many customers. Email systems are contained within several of the sites we have constructed. A built in system like this will perform data base maintenance of your customer list and ensure that the double opt-in system of registration is adhered to. This helps ensure that our customers are compliant with anti-spam rules.

I'm very excited about email campaigns and the potential they hold for retailers as far as lower-cost communication. The process is becoming slightly jaded because of the proliferation of junk and spam emails. If you enter into this realm make sure that your emails are quality and represent something that is worth your readers' time.

We've established and discussed that a percentage of your marketing budget should be ear-marked for digital advertising but what are some of the other alternatives?

It is no secret and I am not the first to recognize or mention that newspapers are struggling given the changing world in which we live. What used to be a good medium with which to communicate to the masses is becoming less so. Dwindling circulations and changes in technologies are causing many local newspapers to become endangered species. This will be entirely dependent, of course, on what resources are available in your trade territory.

Direct mail is an alternative worthy of consideration, but direct mail costs can become substantial. If you choose to use direct mail it is best to increase the odds of the success of your promotion. When deciding who should receive your mailings you will be faced with choices.

For example, the Post Office currently offers a program they call "Every Door Direct Mail". With this program you need no direct mail permit nor do you need an address list. You simply target the neighborhoods you wish to reach, have your mail pieces printed, bundle them as instructed and then deliver them to the post office at the pre-arranged date.

As the name implies the mailing pieces are then delivered to "every door". In fact, delivery goes beyond every door and includes every address on file in the neighborhoods you select. This type of blanketing may work for you. The down side is that you will probably distribute many pieces to addresses that will not be good targets for your offer.

As of this writing the USPS website quotes "prices as low as 14½¢. That certainly appears to be an attractive price. Postcard mailings for example can run upwards of 30¢, with bulk mail rates in the high 20's. But if, for example, you deliver 5,000 pieces where 1250 highly targeted names would have been equally effective, then what appeared to be good value would have changed dramatically after closer inspection.

A company that specializes in direct mail can help you "filter" a list looking for just the right demographic slice for your promotion. For example, you can filter by age, by income, by home-owner/renter and etc. Depending upon the company you're working with, you may have to buy the list, buy if you do you can use it again and again, until you sense that it is obsolete and therefore needs updating.

To determine which system works best for you may take some experimentation. You could try the "Every Door" system a couple times then a direct mail service a couple times and compare your results. Remember, however, the key points of frequency and repetition. That's just fair warning to not give up too soon on anything you might try.

One last point before we leave here (and I could have put this point with any medium), no advertisement can exceed the strength of its offer. If you're planning to advertise a do-hickey for $4.99, for example, and readers are seeing it everywhere else for $3.99, don't advertise it! Advertise only those items on which you can be competitively positioned.

A few years ago I began to think that airwave radio might soon be rendered obsolete too. My thought at the time was: with the proliferation of satellite radios in vehicles and with music streaming in homes, who needs it? I've tempered that opinion somewhat now. I now believe that the medium probably will still wane, its demise is not on the near horizon, however.

Indeed, we have several customers with whom we consult, who still put a large percentage of their advertising funds into radio. Again this will depend upon the local stations from which you have to choose. It is important to match the station format to your target customer.

Choosing your ideal target customer is another discussion and one that we dealt with exhaustively in Discovery-Based

Retail. If you've not gone through the process of identifying your ideal customer and customer demographic, you'll find it worthwhile, and particularly in the context of picking the right advertising mediums. If your target customers are seniors, for example, you probably won't want to spend or focus on Twitter. Conversely, if your targets are the 20-somethings you probably won't benefit from advertising on an AM station that relives the 40's era music.

Before the advent of local cable networks television, advertising was prohibitively expensive for many small to mid-size retailers. However many cable providers now offer bundles that will put your messages on news networks or even nested in sports broadcasts. From what I've seen, some package deals now offered in this medium appear to be very attractive alternatives.

Buy a package that consists of a couple hundred spots and your cable company will come to your store, record footage and produce your 30 or 60 second advertisement. Many look very polished and can really give your store some exposure and sparkle. General informational marketing is not as powerful here as advertisements that have strong offers.

Here are a couple more points about advertising. With all of the mediums we've just discussed, in order for them to be successful they must draw people through space and time.

For example, if I receive a newspaper ad on Saturday evening and your store is closed on Sunday, the ad offer must be strong enough and memorable enough to pull me, not only the distance from my house to your store, but also from Saturday to Monday. If I work on Monday during your open-hours the likelihood of my responding to your promotion will decay with time.

For this reason, although drive-time radio commercials are the priciest they may represent the best value. This too, depends on your individual situation, but if your store sits on a busy commute route, radio listeners could be exposed to your special offer at just the right moment for them to pull in and take advantage.

But what if there was a way to make sure that they heard your offer at just the exact moment they approached your business? Would the advertisement be more powerful? I believe common-sense would almost guarantee this to be so. But there is no way to ensure that, is there?

Obviously with radio advertising that is certainly true. But there is another way--Digital Sign Boards.

Digital signs or messaging boards represent sizable investments. In fact, on the surface, it might seem that their prices would put them out of reach. But upon further examination you might find that these technological marvels represent your best opportunity for continual advertising that meets both the "frequency and repetition" characteristics of successful campaigns.

With digital message boards the issues of time and space are instantly negated. If a driver-by sees your message and is compelled to react to it he has the opportunity to do so at that very moment. "Right turn, Clyde"

I am certainly not the first to realize the impact of this communication medium. Read this excerpt from a compelling article written by the SBA (Small Business Administration):

> "Businesses who added an outdoor LED sign enjoyed typical sales increases of 15%-150%. Not only does an LED Display produce a great return on investment, it costs very little compared to other types of advertising. With an LED sign, the average cost to achieve 1000 impressions (CPT) on consumers as the pass your business is less than 10% of the cost to reach them using any other marketing medium, including TV, radio and newspaper.
>
> For example, a small business that makes $1,000 a day in gross income adds an Outdoor LED sign. The business quickly increases by the minimum of 15%, adding another $150 per day in total revenue. That turns into an additional $1,050.00 a week revenue, or $54,600.00 per year.
>
> Businesses often select their advertising medium, and messages, based upon the CPT (cost per thousand) exposures of their message to the public. On this basis, no other form of advertising comes close to matching the efficiency and cost-effectiveness, dollar for dollar, of an outdoor LED sign:

- Newspapers – On average, the cost is about $7.39 per 1,000 exposures inside a 10-mile circle of the company's position.
- Television – On average, the cost is about $6.26 for 1,000 exposures.
- Radio – About $5.47 for 1,000 exposures.
- New LED display – Less than $0.15 for 1,000 exposures. How? For example, if you invest $10,000.00 on this type of electronic signage, and the usual life span is ten years or more, the amortized cost on a daily basis is about $0.91. Add the daily charges for electricity (approximately $0.20), giving your company a LED sign total expense total of $1.11. If daily vehicle traffic (passing your sign) is 20,000, your cost would be less than $0.15 per 1,000 exposures (counting drivers only)!

The best part is, with an outdoor LED sign, a company doesn't have to care about missing the target audience like TV advertising, becoming yesterday's news, or having costly production costs for modifying or changing the messages, which happens very frequently with TV, radio and newspapers.

With an outdoor LED sign the company owns the advertising form. An outdoor LED sign works 24 hours a day. The LED sign performs as a very solid, *highly visible salesman; attracting new and current customers into the business.*

The medium speaks straight to the potential customer as they pass by the company's location, and the electronic message center makes the company a landmark in the community."

If I'm beginning to sound like a digital sign salesman, well, the truth is that our company does represent a direct-to-dealer sign source. The reason we chose to get involved is that we were absolutely sold on the effectiveness of the medium. Moving forward we expect to see more of this type of advertising. This begs the question: As we see more of the signs will they begin to fade into the landscape? One can drive the Las Vegas strip and see that although the landscape is ablaze with digital signs, they are still very effective at communication...so I doubt it.

Another trend in retail is in-store-digital-communication. I don't know who started it, but Wal-Mart jumped in early in the movement and still uses it today. With this medium, monitors are hung at strategic locations throughout a store. During the stores' open hours the players' messages cycle through presentations which communicate available brands and special offers.

The thing that I really like about this medium is that the messages are playing at the point in time and space in which the billfolds are opened. Therefore it seems that these messages should have the most impact and least resistance to time erosion and travel limitations.

In fact, because of the elements of time and space, it is my belief that generous portions of your communication budget should be centered "at, in or near-store". That would point to devices like the digital signs and interior networks we just discussed as well as banners, signs and interior decor.

How much should one spend on her advertising budget? That's a good question and one to which there is, once again, not a clear-cut answer. Most sources will cite a percentage figure from 2%-5% of gross sales.

There are drawbacks to using a set percentage of sales. First of all it can vary dramatically from category to category. Also it fails to take in to account the maturity of the business. It will take a larger percentage of sales to launch a company than it will take to maintain an established one.

Still, percentage of sales is the accepted method for a "starting-point" to establish an advertising budget. Once you have determined the percentage that you will spend, you will have to figure out how you're going to allot the dollars.

First select your mediums and then determine what percentage of your total advertising budget will go to each form. You now have a yearly figure for each category. We encourage you to not stop there. Compute the percentage that each month's sales has contributed to the yearly sales total when averaged over a five year period. The five-year leveling will moderate any aberrations that may have occurred due to severe weather or other abnormal conditions.

Once you have the monthly sales percentages figured, take the yearly budget that you established in the first step, perform some quick multiplication and you'll have a monthly advertising budget for each medium you have chosen.

Having your monthly advertising budget pre-established is of great help in keeping you on track with your overall profit goals. When, for example, an advertising salesman comes in with his latest-greatest promotion, you can simply check your "open-to-spend" against his medium. You'll instantly know whether it's something you can do, should you be so inclined.

Advertising and marketing are not necessarily fun expenditures. Most retailers look upon advertising cash outlays as necessary evil expenses rather than investments. Perhaps you do too. If so, you may find it helpful to focus on (you already know) the fact that advertising is one of the most important drivers of retail businesses.

We are often called in to consult with "struggling" retailers. Invariably we find that advertising and marketing funds have been dramatically pared as a reaction to low sales and tough times.

Unfortunately, this often causes a quicker spiral downward. If the advertising efforts have been ineffective, the better course of action is usually reexamination and redirection of funds.

An important thing to remember is that you must have your store ready for customers *before* you advertise. My partner often tells customers that it's not much different than making sure your house is clean and presentable before you invite guests over. I think he's right. Review the other chapters of this book, get your house in order and then invite guests.

5. Employees and Teamwork

There is really no more important consideration in retail stores than employees. As you review your P&L on a monthly basis you'll be reminded of exactly how important it is to leverage payroll cost, which is one of your largest expenditures.

In the past, when speaking to groups, I have presented a program that I called "Increasing your Employee Productivity Gap". It was based on a simple premise: In order for an employee to be a good investment he must produce profit above and beyond the totals of his salary and benefits. The additional dollars between what he produced and what he was paid, I referred to as the Productivity Gap.

It looked good on paper, and I believe it was an interesting presentation, but after more study and consideration, I have come to the conclusion that it misses one very important point. Employees who are members of teams actually develop synergies that go beyond the abilities and capacities of single members. Unfortunately we regularly encounter groups of employees who are certainly not parts of teams. The concept of team is foreign to those groups and that is a failing of management. We'll talk more about that later.

The concept of the employee productivity gap that I mentioned, however, is still valid. It speaks to production per employee and that's an important ratio to monitor. But to evaluate one person's actions and then try to quantify his singular effort to the bottom line result is difficult. Commission based sales people are an exception.

One of the problems store managers encounter as their staff matures and develops tenure with the company is naturally escalating payroll costs. Over the years even small incremental increases can result in shocking payroll numbers.

If sales continued to increase indefinitely, then payroll as a percentage of sales might stay in balance and remain manageable. Unfortunately during economic downturns, our country's financial crisis, for example, those same managers may have found payroll percentages running rampant.

Yearly salary increases over long periods of time are not necessarily bad things. In fact it is often the pinnacle to which owners and managers aspire. They feel compelled to provide for those who are making their success possible and believe in a "share-the-wealth" philosophy.

As I mentioned it can be a shock to wake up and find that what once worked with payroll is no longer possible and payroll as a percentage of sales is now out of balance.

In the case of over-extended payroll and if the top line cannot be increased, then tough decisions must follow. We have witnessed dramatic changes in this regard brought about by the economic slow-down. Employers who once picked up all or large portions of insurance premiums, for example, have pared those percentages way back, some being forced to retract them completely. As the government continues to mandate changes this may become an even taller hurdle for small enterprises.

Along with the paring of benefits we've seen some stores experiment with cutting hours and even days from working schedules. Changes forced by payrolls which are out of control are not pleasant and no one wants their business to come to that. Still, realities dictate that the manager ride expenses like a wild horse until they are tamed and brought under control.

Since all of the points I have discussed thus far fall under the category of "I don't want to go there", let's examine some steps that may help you avoid similar situations in the future.

I mentioned the importance of team within a retail setting. Staff which function well as a team invariably produce more sales per employee than one that doesn't. But a team does not develop on its own and without guidance. Let's start with some basic principles.

I like the point Jim Collins made in his book titled "From Good to Great". I am paraphrasing here but you'll capture the essence: *The destination of your bus may, probably will, change over time. (In this case the bus is your retail store.) It is most important then that you have the right people on the bus.*

My interpretation of this is: regardless of the varied tasks that might lie ahead, the quality of the individuals that you have to assign to those tasks should be a constant you can rely on.

As we have worked with stores through the years we have observed that each one has a prevailing attitude. Some stores have a *"we love our jobs, and we're here to serve, whatever it takes"* attitude. Employees of these stores sincerely like what they're doing and derive personal fulfillment from their tasks.

Other stores, it seems, develop more of an *"it's not my job, I don't know whose job it is, and I don't really care"* attitude. Look at the faces and observe the demeanor of employees in these stores and you'll just feel dissatisfaction oozing from the pores. I'll give you odds on which store you'd be attracted to.

How does a store develop a negative attitude? Why aren't the powers-that-be aware of it? And why don't they change it? Those are good questions and are worth consideration.

Let's look first at *how it happens*. It is my belief, substantiated through observation, that attitudes are contagious…contagious, just as surely as colds and flu are contagious. Furthermore I am quite convinced that attitudes most often start at the top and are assimilated downward.

This already gives us insight as to why managers are sometimes unaware of the problem. If the problem does originate with them, it may be engrained so deeply that they've become unable to sense it. If the bad attitudes start at a mid-point and flow downward, perhaps the manager is simply unaware of it. Others may be but for whatever reason are unwilling to deal with it. Still some, I suppose, are just unaware of how important the collective attitude of their stores is.

Perhaps the owner or manager feels that if they bring in a good selection of product, present it and price it right, that attitude falls way down on the list of their customers' considerations.

If there are those people, I believe them to be dead wrong. There are just too many choices: too many stores with good selections of products, too many stores with great presentation and competitive prices. I have stated many times that we have witnessed retail stores fail for several reasons but the failure to manage employee costs and employee teams are near the top of that list.

One condition that should make it easier for employers as of this writing is the high-unemployment rate that exists in many parts of the country. On the surface it would seem that qualified applicants would be clamoring for employment opportunities. From the managers we've dealt with, however, it seems that such is not the case.

For those looking for new hires here are a few thoughts on where to begin your search. When I was very young and working as a delivery person for a lumber yard in a mid-sized community I was approached, while on the job, by a gentleman who owned a lawn and garden nursery. He explained that he had observed me working with customers and had liked what he had seen. He went on to tell me that he was looking for someone he could groom to fill a manager position within his company. When he asked how much I was making he told me that he could immediately increase my pay significantly and offer me a brighter future. As it turned out I was planning to leave the community soon and therefore turned down his offer.

There are a few points that have always struck me about that encounter. He was not concerned whether or not I had experience in his field. In fact, he probably correctly assumed that I didn't. He was tuned in completely to customer experience. I have no idea what he had observed me doing that he liked, but apparently he saw qualities that he thought would fit well in his business. He didn't wait for job seekers to come to him and fill out an application. He observed employed people in their daily tasks and selected, it seems, from that group. That doesn't seem like a bad idea to me.

He could have taken an attitude something like: *my business is very specialized and, therefore, I want someone who has experience in my field.* Instead he chose to prioritize good customer experience over background.

I have read it suggested that one should "hire for attitude and train for skills". When it comes to retail and hiring staff, I believe this to be a great guide. Of course, the position itself would be a determining factor.

I mentioned that I took management training with the T.G. & Y stores early on in my career. They hired people from varying backgrounds and, as I recall, retail experience was not a requirement. When they selected candidates to enter their training programs the curriculum was very orchestrated and comprehensive. The training was married with mentoring programs which included working side by side with Store Mangers, Co-Managers and Assistant Managers. Once you had completed the formal training you were promoted to assistant manager and worked in that capacity until you were promoted to co-manager. In this way, the company kept a conduit full of trained replacements to fill vacancies left by terminations, retirements, and new store opportunities.

Within the industry that I have spent most of my working career, (the hardware store and home center industry) independent store owners have boasted through the years that they have an edge in customer service. At one time that may have been the case.

What I observe today, however, is that the giant store formats have closed these gaps considerably, if not completely. In fact it seems that I am just as likely, or more likely, to be able to talk to an expert in one of the big box departments as I am the corner hardware store.

What happened? I believe that independents were resting on laurels and past successes. As they listened to the stories of how lousy the competitions' customer service was, those same competitors were implementing systems to improve things.

Consider this right now. You bring a new employee into your store. You have recruited her through some device and she now sits in your office. Do you have a thorough system to bring her up to speed? Do you have manuals that include basic store policy requirements that she must test out of, so that you are assured she comprehends? Do you have someone who will work side by side with her to show her what is expected? Do you have an extended training program in place to take her from where she is now to where you want her to be? Do you have schedules and systems to train her in product knowledge? Do you have systems in place to train her how to merchandise for profit? Do you have systems that will assure she understands what is expected of her regarding store maintenance?

If you acknowledge that these systems are not in place, you have work to do. During our consultative visits we have had many opportunities to interact with employees. We are often blown away by employees who have a year or more on the job and are still operating in a fog due to a lack of orchestrated training. When these employees fail or become disillusioned with their position, it is not necessarily their faults. It takes work to grow great employees.

Remember my theory on the giant thinking head that seems to mandate large chain store operations? I mentioned how all of the systems flow down to the stores beneath. Employee training is a perfect example of dissemination of such systems. When training is a system and the system works, all is well. When training is sporadic, unscheduled and irregular it will almost certainly fail.

It should go without saying that some of the material will have to be written at store level, but it would be unfair to ask a manager of any store to author all of the necessary training materials to bring about the desired results. It is not unfair, however, to ask her to determine which training materials the store will use, purchase those materials, schedule their use and then implement compliance requirements.

There are many resources that can be explored on the Internet. Perhaps you have suppliers that make available training resources too. The resources are rarely free, but once again this is an area in which it is critical that you view the expenditures as investments rather than expenses.

Employee training is something that must be ongoing. You are never at the top of the hill with this discipline. There are a few reasons for this important point. Consider these: (1) Products are always changing or evolving. What you knew yesterday may not be entirely accurate today. (2) Sales skills and industry accepted practices change over time too. It is important that you are personally aware of these changes and then disseminate the information to your staff in whatever you deem to be an appropriate manner. (3) Personal growth is an important quality in determining whether employees are happy with their jobs. To continue to engage and educate your staff will offset what you may not be able to otherwise compensate.

This discussion on an educational process for your employees has focused on individual improvement. We haven't, however discussed the collective mentality and synergies that develop a sense of team and teamwork. I mentioned just a moment ago how individual education serves as a reward and perceived compensation for many people in the form of self-improvement. A feeling of being part of a team is an equally powerful incentive which can promote long-term service from employees.

Store meetings are great and important ways to foster feelings of team and teamwork. They can have the additional benefit of being part of an ongoing educational plan. In order for store meetings to contribute to these worthwhile goals, however, they must be thoroughly planned and orchestrated.

Each meeting should have an agenda and specific goals. We have had managers tell us that they conduct regular store meetings. And yet when we asked about the content of those meetings, the managers admitted them to be ill-planned, if planned at all. Apparently they hoped by opening the times up to question and answer sessions the meetings would magically develop legs and walk on their own.

Other managers have told us that with their other responsibilities, planning store meetings just seem to fall through the cracks. We fully acknowledge that managing a store is demanding. Sometimes within the scope of those demands, compromises must be made. However, given the importance of employees and the crucial profit ratio that production per employee represents, perhaps this should be a last consideration for compromise.

Here are a few suggestions for organizing and conducting store meetings. First realize that the entire meeting is not your responsibility. Staff may not want to listen to you drone on for 30-45 minutes. In fact, you'll learn that if you assign various presentation points to other employees, they will feel as if they've been entrusted with something very important because they have. Their assignments will require them to prepare and be well-versed with whatever you've assigned them. This is a good thing and part of their educational process.

Staff members are more likely to be engaged by presentations by their peers. They are more likely to ask questions and interact with them too. Your presence serves as a patrol to help prevent things taking wrong turns, but do allow the staff to express opinions and question one another.

For example, if you were managing a hardware store, you might ask Molly to make a presentation about a new line of paint brushes. Molly would be required to read, study, and learn about the line in order to successfully present it. The preparation would serve as a perfect dress rehearsal for her to later present the products and their advantages to customers.

Notice all of the positives that have happened through this process. Molly was required to learn. While sharing what she learned she has helped to train her peers. She has had the opportunity to present to a group, thereby performing a type of dress-rehearsal for sales presentations. And finally she has been made to feel important because of the task that was assigned her. Now in the same meeting or a next one, assign the responsibility of teaching the staff about the new line of ...well, you fill in the blank, to Bobby, and then to Alex and then to...you get the picture.

It would be the responsibility of whoever was placed in charge of the meeting to organize the presentation tasks. But beyond that, the store meeting responsibilities would be shared.

The meetings should not stop with product knowledge education, obviously. During these meetings the person in charge should continue to educate personnel as regards merchandising for profit. Some of the things that you learned in the earlier chapters of this book, for example would be great lessons to share with your staff. It may also serve as impetus to encourage you and your key personnel to continue their education process.

Store policies and procedures should be continually reinforced during these get-togethers. Store meetings can also serve as an ideal time to fortify understanding of the promotions you may be running. For example:

> "OK, everybody, we've got this circular coming out on Thursday. You should have all of the merchandise on the floor by now, but please double-check.
>
> Let's review the front page, that's where our margins are the smallest. We need to come up with some things to display beside the sale items that

will make great add-on sales to the featured products."

.....And then, after some give and take with the staff....

"We've got some great ideas on add-on products now, please brush up on the items we chose so that you can sell them effectively. We'll probably ask some impromptu questions about them as we walk by. We have to make sure that we sell the add-on items so we can protect our margins during the promotion.

Also, Sarah, will you please use your magical computer skills to print up some signs telling people why they should purchase the add-on items?

One last thing, make sure we're ready for guests. Get your departments in tip-top shape. Some of the people who will be coming in with their circulars will never have seen our stores before. We want to make good impressions."

We have seen remarkable results in stores that conduct regular store meetings. Store employees who feel engaged always show a higher satisfaction level with their jobs. Store meetings are a great way of fostering feelings of being part of something worthwhile...part of a team.

Earlier I mentioned that attitudes seem to permeate downward. I also mentioned that although that decay sometimes starts at the top, it is also true that sometimes it starts at intermediate positions instead. The first part of correcting any problem is recognizing that there is one.

Unfortunately, recognizing the problem does not necessarily lead to its resolution. We once worked with a store in which the manager had a great and positive attitude toward improving the customer experience in his store. We suggested many physical changes to his store's environment. He implemented them and they proved to be positive.

The primary Achilles Heel in this store was one person...one person in a staff of several. The problem was that this employee had worked for the company for a number of years. Sometime during that period and for whatever reason, he developed a cancerous attitude. I'm assuming he developed the bad attitude over time. It makes no sense to me otherwise. If his manager had observed bad behavior during the early days of the employee's tenure I can't imagine that it would have been allowed to continue.

It manifested itself in several ways. He was short and borderline rude when he dealt with customers. The staff that answered to him seemed to reflect his mannerisms. As if that weren't bad enough, when an employee tried to operate outside of the patterns he had established, that employee was derided until he eventually joined the ranks of the bad-apple supervisor.

After observing his behavior and that of those who were forced to answer to him we broached the subject with the manager. During that conversation the manager acknowledged that he was aware of the supervisor's attitude. He rationalized, however, that his non-actions of addressing the situation were justified by pointing out that the employee knew things that others just didn't know. He further commented how reliable the guy was and reemphasized how long he had been with the company.

He elected to retain the employee, saying that he would coach him. It never happened. The business continued to flounder although many elements of success were in place. Unfortunately, the store did not survive.

I'm not stating that one person led to the company's demise. I would state without qualification, however that the manager's non-action in this very real problem was one of the contributing factors.

When you examine your staff, member by member, be realistic in your evaluations. If you are aware that you have problems, devise a plan to address those problems. Assign dates for the completion of the steps you deem necessary to correct them.

Sometimes problem employees can be reeducated, sometimes they can't. Often, what you observe as problems are deep-seated personality quirks. There are people who have the ability to interact with other employees and customers. You want those people on your staff.

Working through employees that are holding your operation back is not a pleasant task. If your store is going to reach its potential, however, it is a necessary one.

Whether you have openings created through this process or openings created by growing business there are some steps that you will find helpful in screening for new employees.

Sit down and consider all of the responsibilities you want the new employee to shoulder. It will be a good idea to also consider the percentages of time the employee will be assigned to various tasks. If, for example, the employee will spend 70% of their time checking in freight and otherwise processing orders you will be looking for a different personality type than if you are asking them to interact with customers 70% of the time.

Once you have a strong idea what you expect of the new hire, consider current staff members. If any of them are excelling in similar job descriptions, document the personality traits that you believe to be contributing to their success. You will then have a blueprint to follow. If you know exactly who you're looking for during the hiring process you'll more likely have success.

The next step you should take is to formulate a clear "sales" strategy. You are seeking out the best possible candidate, whatever the available position. If you are going to get the best, it may involve communicating to that person that you are offering her a great opportunity. What are the attributes of the available job particularly and working for your company in general that should make it attractive to her? If you have trouble here, that may signal that you've got some issues to work through. It begs the question: if you offer a job that, as an employer, you view having little potential, why would she?

The attributes that I'm speaking of need not be things like

- Unlimited growth opportunities.
- Quarterly raises.
- 2 Weeks paid vacation.
- Retirement packages.
- Full medical and dental.

If you're offering those, give me a call.

Here are some less spectacular job attributes that candidates may find attractive.

- Flexible work schedules
- Casual Fridays
- Fun team outings
- Company shirts or smocks
- Special company reward bucks

The important thing to remember is that if you think you've got a menial job that offers little personal reward to the candidates they may sense that and walk away with the same feeling. Just be prepared to *sell* your great opportunity.

After you have completed this process you'll now be ready to actively search out job candidates. I mentioned earlier the guy who, years ago, tried to hire me away from a completely unrelated industry. I don't think that's a bad idea. If you observe someone on the job when they're completely unaware of your intentions you will definitely see her in her natural behavior. Of course, you'd simply ask her to come in for an interview if you wanted to take the next step. You want to have more than one candidate from which to choose.

I have had some employers tell me that if they have a great employee they will ask that person whether they know someone who is looking for a job. The assumption here is that similar personalities run together and it might lead to another ringer. In addition, if the current great employee is happy in their position, that would be communicated to the prospect as well.

Advertising a position is usually necessary to have the largest pool of potential candidates from which to choose. Local newspaper may work but remember that the ad will connect with only those who are in close proximity.

There are many websites that you can advertise job openings for little or no costs. The big advantage of these resources beyond the low cost is that they are not limited by geography. You never know… someone who might be a perfect fit for your opportunity may be looking to relocate to your town.

One more point worth mentioning is advertising to a specific audience…a college in your community, for example. If you find a recruit who is interested in retail, that part-time position filler may develop to be the manager of your next location.

Once the resumes start coming in, sort them into two groups: the ones you want to explore and the ones, that for whatever reasons, you don't.

Call the candidates yourself. This will give you one more time to interact with them and gage your perceptions. Schedule interviews with as many candidates as possible within a condensed time range. If the interviews are all fresh in your mind you'll have an easier time contrasting them.

It's a good idea to narrow down your selections to 2 or 3. Once that is done you can call those candidates back for second interviews. It might be beneficial to have your most key employee participate in the interview this time and get her impressions of the final group. She will probably be working closely with the new employee and may observe something that eludes you.

Have your interview questions formulated. You can find some great suggestions online. Remember to interview with purpose. Predetermine what you hope to learn about the candidates and then pick questions you think will give you insight into those qualities. Interviewing is never an exact science. If it were no one would ever fail in a job. That aside, however, it still makes sense to know what you're trying to learn and have a plan for doing so.

Once you have made a decision, act quickly. There is no need to have wasted the time and efforts spent for the interview process only to learn that your favorite applicant took a job with another company. Make an offer, see how it sits, negotiate if necessary, and complete the deal.

I want to emphasize one more time because it is of the highest importance, to make sure you have her training completely pre-orchestrated. She may have ideal attributes, yet still fail miserably if she is inadequately trained.

The take-away from this week's study is that you must perform an honest evaluation of your staff. If there are problems with an employee, you must make the tough decision whether to cut your losses now or guide him through a rehabilitation process. If you choose the latter, monitor the progress and set time goals for observable improvements. If you decide that he is not salvageable begin the search for his replacement.

Remember, which ever course you choose, you are offering a tremendous opportunity. As I said, it will take tough decisions, but hey, that's why you're paid the big bucks...right?

6. Scratching a Niche

Understanding how your store fits in to the market within which it operates is a discussion of "store slotting" and as I stated earlier, we covered that thoroughly in our book, Discovery-Based Retail. If you don't understand slotting, please pick up a copy and bring yourself up to speed on those concepts. I recently had a call from a gentleman who wanted to thank us for writing that book. He shared that he thought the chapter on slotting had helped him more than any other in understanding his unique situation.

Understanding what your store is, before you understand how it fits in to your arena, may be even more important and perhaps should have been discussed before slotting. Well, we didn't do it that way. The more we work with retailers in consulting capacities the more we become enlightened to things that can potentially go wrong.

One thing that we have noticed is retailers' hesitation to go outside of their store definition. Because I have many years in the hardware industry, I will again use a hardware store as an example.

When hardware stores are originally set, they follow traditional ideas and consist of the usual core departments. In a hardware store, the core departments are electrical, tools and power tools, plumbing, fasteners, builders' hardware, lawn and garden etc. The departments are usually a reflection of the store's primary distributor's inventories. (If yours is a clothing store, for example, think men's wear, ladies' wear, lingerie, shoes, etc.)

In the case of the hardware industry and tradition, the old tried-and-true layout serves as a great starting point for launching a store. However, there comes a point in time when the productivity of the store needs to be evaluated to determine if the traditional departments are producing at rates commensurate with the inventories and spaces allotted them.

We have observed that many store owners and managers have failed to analyze this information or if they did, they failed to act upon on what they learned. Others may have determined that a department is failing to meet its productivity expectations and may have even tried various changes. If those changes failed to energize the department, it still sits there, digesting inventory, staffing and the other resources that dead departments consume.

When we analyze how various departments are performing within the stores with which we consult we strive for optimum ratios. A department that is performing anemically steals opportunity from other departments. This could be characterized as producing "opportunity costs".

A simple example of opportunity cost goes like this. I go into a restaurant unsure of what to order. I look at the menu and vacilate between the steak and chicken. I consider my choices, visualize both and ultimately choose to order the chicken. After my meal is served and I am eating the chicken I see the waiter serve another customer the steak and it looks beyond awesome! I now have two costs invested in my meal. I have the real money I have to pay for the chicken but I also have the opportunity cost, which is that I can't have the steak because I already have the chicken.

That's a simple story and in the case of a meal it wouldn't be a huge deal. I would simply remember my experience and order steak the next time. When you consider it closely, you'll see that in a very real sense this is a great lesson for retailers of all sorts.

In my hardware store example the chicken might be analogous to my electrical department. I already have the electrical department and I have tried for a couple years to make it earn its salt and still it doesn't. Its performance is dismal. The space is filled, the dollars spent, and the dead area continues to "steal" from me each and every day.

Let's say that I suddenly see a wonderful opportunity in...well, you fill in the blank...we'll say home theater for this discussion. As I just stated the resources I might be able to allot to the opportunity are already chewed up. They're invested in my lousy electrical department.

What usually happens at this point is a thought process something like this. Mine is a hardware store. A hardware store always has an electrical department. It's traditional. If I chose to give up my electrical department I would no longer be a hardware store. If I had a home theater department instead, what would my store be? I must be off my rocker. And the idea is dismissed.

There are a couple different points that I need to emphasize. Perhaps somewhere between having no electrical department and what I currently have is a ratio that will work. It is a matter of computing how many sales dollars (or margin dollars) per square foot the department is producing relative to the rest of the store. If I can keep the best sellers from the department, close out the dogs, and condense the departmental footprint, I'll have something to reevaluate in six months. At that time I may find that the new streamlined department is producing at a ratio that works. The space that I freed through the process could be allotted to departments that are producing well already or maybe to brand new opportunities...my home theater department for example.

But let's say for discussion that even after these moves the new condensed electrical department isn't working. This assumes that I had already done my homework and was certain that product mix and pricing were not my problems. What now?

As I mentioned earlier to cut an electrical department from a hardware store would be frightening wouldn't it? One might wrestle with an identity crisis. I guess, for me, it boils down to this question. Do I really want a traditional hardware store or do I want a non-traditional store that's considerably more profitable?

Stores often go through evolutionary processes...starting out as one thing making their way to something entirely different. These may be cases of astute managers following a credo of "do what you do do well."

Let me site an example of how this metamorphoses might occur. We'll continue with my hardware store and electrical department example.

Bill is the manager of a hardware store just like we've been discussing. He had an anemically performing electrical department. He studied competition, found his prices to be very competitive, his assortments to be comparable and yet the results were abysmal. He reasoned that the two electrical wholesalers which were in close proximity were dominating that business segment.

He elected to pare his department way back and devote additional space to his lawn and garden department which was already performing well.

Bill had never carried lawn mowers and string trimmers but was strong in fertilizer, seed and bedding plants. He also did well with patio heaters, grills and accessories. Mowers seemed like a natural extension. He researched and found a high profile brand that didn't have strong distribution in his market.

With the space he gained from condensing his electrical department he showcased the new line of mowers. They took off immediately and begin selling far beyond his expectations. Before long he realized that he needed even more room to show more models and set up a service counter. Where should he get the space? The obvious choice was to discontinue what was left of the floundering electrical department.

Bill continued to grow his lawn and garden business. And eventually what was once a floundering "Bill's Hardware" was now a dynamic and flourishing "Bill's Lawn, Garden and Mower Emporium".

This is a fictional story, but over and over we've seen similar story lines play out. Bill had the vision and the intestinal fortitude to make some really tough decisions and ultimately profited greatly from them.

I'm not suggesting that you modify your store to this degree unless you've already gone through several steps of investigation and evaluation.

There are several elements that can improve the performance of individual departments. Let's talk about those for a while. You'll notice as we discuss these elements they run hand-in-hand identical to the 6 Ps of differentiation. Why is that?

The answer should be pretty obvious, but what we're trying to do is differentiate our individual departments just as surely as we're trying to differentiate our entire store. So, if it helps, you can think about it as if you've got 6 or 8, or whatever the number, stores within your store.

Interestingly, "store within a store" was a term coined a number of years back to describe giving one department special treatment to make it stand above other departments. It's a good and effective concept, but it seems that it's also a good way to evaluate all of the individual departments and become a "super sleuth" as to ways to improve them. Improve the pieces and you will, no doubt, improve the whole.

So we'll take a department and I guess we'll continue using the sub-performing electrical department as our example and filter it through the 6 Ps. We'll just go down the list and see how the system can help us locate problems and identify opportunities. Within your store, whatever the offering, select a department and do the same.

The first P, you'll remember is proximity. Within the store, drilling down to departmental level, proximity refers to locations within the layout. This is critical and especially in the case of a store in which traffic does not typically navigate the entire area. As I mentioned in an earlier chapter this is often the failure or shortcoming of a bad layout. So that has to be a consideration in this discussion as well.

For now, we'll assume that your store has a good layout. So the question becomes would you be better off showcasing the anemic department nearer the front of the store? Regardless of how good the store's layout actually is, the front area of any store is exposed to the greatest amount of traffic. This is without exception.

There are departments within every store type that by virtue of the product itself will draw people to the farthest points. This is why the produce, milk and eggs are always on the perimeter of a grocery store. Shoppers will seek out these items, which thereby draws them through and exposes them to the rest of the store.

In a hardware store the fastener department works this way. A well thought out hardware store will have the fasteners located deep in the store. This will pull customers past other merchandise making them more likely to shop other departments.

So within the context of this discussion, consider the department that you are evaluating and conceptualize all you would gain and what you might lose by its relocation. Also within your examination of the department's location, consider whether the departments that are adjacent make sense. Are there natural transitions to the neighboring departments? Proximity--it is important at an inner-store level.

The second P of differentiation is People. The quality and training of those who staff certain departments are even more crucial than others. For example, in an electrical department, qualified staff is paramount. I've noticed that some Home Depot stores now have signs up that state their departments are manned by master-electricians. I'll throw the question up to you. If you were a do-it-yourselfer looking for answers to questions and supplies for a project would you go to a store where you could find professional help or to one staffed by part-timers? The answer is obvious for an electrical project, but as I stated earlier different departments will have different staffing requirements.

It should go without saying, but I'll reinforce it just the same. I'm using examples from the hardware and home center industries. It doesn't matter! Fill in your department name, evaluate the expertise it takes to staff it...your shoe department, for example, or your produce department, whatever. The facts are the facts and facts will be consistent for any type of retail. Staff any department with more skilled employees than does your competitor and you will gain a differentiating edge.

Before we leave the P that represents people, remember to consider that personality qualities, like friendliness and willingness to help also enter into this discussion. Even if you've got an expert on staff, if his attitude is abrasive and venomous, customers will likely go elsewhere.

The next P that will differentiate a department from competitors is presentation. I mentioned that a few years ago the phrase "store within a store" was coined. I also mentioned that it referred to an area within a store that was separated, usually by different floor treatments, more upscale décor, and perhaps a change in color. The idea was to make this area a focal point. It's easy to spot these departments. For example a ready-to-wear store may have a vinyl tiled floor throughout, until you get to the shoe department. The change to carpet there accomplishes a couple things. Of course, it assures that the bottoms of shoes stay clean and new looking even though they have been tried on and walked in. But beyond that, and more importantly, it makes that area of the operation look more like a free-standing shoe store.

This simple change in presentation allows the ready-to-wear store to take on another identity. The idea here is that psychologically the whole store now has broader appeal. The store may not be large enough to be considered a destination store for ready-to-wear (see store-slotting Discovery-Based Retail), Given the size of some free-standing competitors however, it may be able to create the appeal of a destination shoe store and accomplish this all under the original roof.

I've seen stores and you probably have too, with this "store within a store" concept using multiple departments. It creates a very appealing environment. The more appealing a store's environment, the more shoppers it will have. The more appealing an environment, the longer customers will shop and likely spend more. The more appealing an environment, the greater the chances the store will enjoy longer employee retention. I could go on here, I'm on a roll, but I'll spare you. Suffice it to say that how a department looks is important to its success. The P that is presentation is critical to all departments of your store.

The next P of differentiation, promotion, also still applies at a departmental level. Promotion, in this case, could be advertising, of course. It can also be things as simple as communicative signage within the department.

Let's take a lesson from the Home Depot operation that I mentioned earlier. Remember I said they had at least one staff member who was a master electrician. How did I know that? Did I just sense it or clairvoyantly receive it? Nope, nothing that dramatic, I assure you. The fact is they had several signs posted that just came right out and said it.

If they would not have used these signs, which represented the "P" that is promotion, the positive personnel changes that had been made would have gone unnoticed. Because they took the simple step of making signs, even though I was not in the market for anything electrical, it sure made an impression on me. So just imagine how the message would have thrilled someone looking for good answers.

Remember promotion can be very simple stuff and is directly related to marketing. Communicate and steer your brand!

10 Weeks to a Better Retail Operation

7. Pricing and Margin

A gentleman who I worked with several years ago, and whom I had great respect for once talked to me about price. He and I were salespeople representing a hardware wholesaler at the time. We were struggling with a customer whose business we were about to lose to a much larger and formidable competitor. We had gotten our act together, honed our presentation, and made one last effort to retain the customer.

At dinner, while reviewing how it had gone, Jack made a statement that has really stuck with me. Not necessarily because it was accurate, for I don't believe it to be completely so, but, rather, because it was so laser-focused. During our post-meeting get-together I was lamenting the fact that the other company was larger, had more attractive programs, and wider selections of products.

"You forgot price, but price isn't just another thing," he said, "It's the only thing."

We were involved in wholesale, your store is retail. And as I mentioned I don't believe price to be the "only thing", but the way that statement and that story drills down on the importance of price makes it worth considering.

How do you establish your retail prices without being cognizant of what your competitors are doing? The short answer is...you don't. It takes work. It takes price shops and it takes repetition. You won't fully know where your prices stand against competitors after one price shop or two. Pricing in your market place is dynamic and, therefore, its examination must be on-going.

Once you have determined where your competitors are priced you must then plot a strategy to ensure that customers view your prices as acceptable while maintaining adequate margins to justify your investment.

This is done through a strategy referred to as variable pricing. The idea of variable pricing is to sell items that people are more price aware of, the "price-sensitive items" at narrower margins. The rationale is that the other items, items which are not as price-sensitive, are less likely noticed when their prices are increased. If the system functions properly, a balance is achieved. Customers' pricing perceptions of the store are acceptable and better margins are generated.

As customers have become more aware of systems like this and as it has become easier to research prices via the Internet, things have become more complex. What was once a single line of demarcation...either price sensitive or not, has turned into several layers of sensitivity codes and corresponding margins with the individual layers.

What makes an item more price-sensitive? Here are some influencing attributes.

- Higher ticket items are more price-sensitive.
- Items less than a dollar or even five dollars now are much less so.
- Items which are purchased frequently and therefore are at top-level consciousness are more price-sensitive.
- Items that are advertised frequently.
- Items which are available in more area stores will be more price sensitive.
- Name brand items may be more price sensitive the private-branded items.

If you want to use a variable pricing strategy in your store, you must choose how many levels of price codes you want to deal with. In certain businesses your vendor may have already done this. If so, you're probably familiar with variable pricing strategies and your job will be easier.

If not, like I said, pick your number of layers, use guidelines like those above and assign a layer number to each item in your store. Hopefully you'll have an open field on your point-of-sale system to contain yet another number.

Start with a department, print sales by item after you have assigned the new field. Compare the margins of the various items within each layer that you established. Now calculate and determine what number would allow you to level margins across that layer. You may notice some items that you need to move to the layer above or below to make one margin per layer work. The idea is that each item in every layer is priced using the same margin.

The goal of this process, which by the way will be difficult, is to allow you the benefit of being able to move a single margin across layers to react to competitive changes. It will also make price checks easier, and help you to squeeze out incremental margin improvements.

After a time on your newly established system you could readily compute what would happen if you changed margins on given layers. For example, what how would it impact your store's margin if you lowered your Sensitivity Layer 1 items, (your most price-sensitive) from a 30% margin (remember, they're all the same now) to 20% to put forth a more competitive image? And if you did that, could you maintain your overall margin if you raised your Sensitivity Level 5 items (this would be your most blind items if you established 5 levels) by 5%?

It will take some experimentation to get through the process. But once you do, you'll feel more in control of your pricing image and margin.

In Discovery-Based Retail, I mentioned that you should imagine a glass ceiling on pricing. The idea is to press right up against the glass ceiling (what your market will bear) but not to break it. Once the ceiling is broken, your store is viewed as "too high-priced". When that happens it is difficult and costly to reverse the negative image.

I debated about even bringing up the question of how margin is figured. However, we have talked to several dealers who did not understand the distinction between margin and markup. Therefore I decided to cover it briefly.

If you have a strong grasp on the difference please scan ahead.

When you deal with your profit and loss and when you compare your figures to industry averages or prepare reports for your bank, you'll always be dealing with margin.

Let's assume that an item costs $1.00. If I multiply $1.00 times 1.5 and end up with a retail of $1.50 I will have a 50 cent profit. Fifty cents is one-third of $1.50, therefore my margin is 33.33% (one-third) of the sale price. Even though we had a markup of 50%, *the margin we realized is only 33.33%.*

Here's a simple way to figure a retail price for the margin you want to make. Let's say that you want to realize 40% margin. First subtract 40% from 100%. Your remainder will by 60%. Now divide your cost by 60%. Let's use our $1.00 cost example again.

Divide $1.00 by 60% and you'll get $l.67. Sell your item for $1.67 and you'll make .67 cents. Sixty seven cents is 40% of $1.67. You made a 40% <u>margin</u>.

I know there are other ways to compute margin, but this is the one I was originally taught and the one I still use. The important thing is that you realize that margin and markup are different.

Maintaining margins is one the most difficult tasks for many store managers. Others seem to have a knack for it and no problems at all. Let's look at a few things that can either erode or improve the margin in your store.

1. <u>Failure to rotate stock</u>. This is a simple concept. All you have to do is place the new items that come in behind the older stock of the same item. Even if your items are non-perishables and seem to have unlimited shelf life, it's important. Packages tend to yellow and fade with time. Fail to rotate your stock and someday soon you'll be marking down a package or two just because they look bad. Mark downs, whatever the reasons, kill margins.

2. <u>Buy better.</u> This obvious point is often overlooked and is probably because of habits. We habitually call the same source for product without giving consideration as to whether the source offers us the best deal. Even if vendor prices were compared at one time it makes sense to verify them occasionally. Of course you don't want a ton of time exhausted to price shop each time you buy.

   That said there is an experience from my past that should alert you. Before I was promoted to Vice-President of sales with a hardware distributor, I was a salesperson for the company for many years. Most of my competitors operated above-board. There was one, however, that would come in offering programs far beyond what I or others were able to match. Unfortunately for the customers who switched, the sneaky vendor's pricing was always changed shortly thereafter. Those who caught the shift either fought for the pricing that was quoted and monitored it weekly or decided they wanted to do business with someone they could trust and returned to their original vendors. As an aside, this company is still out there and from what I've been told still operates this way.

The reason buying right is important to margin should be readily apparent, but here are a couple of cautions. Many vendors have different levels of pricing based upon the amount of yearly volume you do with them. If you are using two or more suppliers to buy products that are available from either, it may be to your benefit to explore committing all of the business to one or the other. A total volume commitment may get you to next level pricing. This move can also decrease many of your processing costs. For example, it will take less time and therefore cost less to place an order with one vendor instead of two. It will take less time and therefore cost less to receive and process orders from one vendor too.

Here is another important point. If you are able to successfully "buy down" your cost by combining purchases, and if your current retails are working, absorb the lowered cost to increase your margin.

If, however you continue to use your pricing model (current margin targets) with a lower cost you will not increase your margin, but you will decrease your margin dollars. So be careful.

Here's what I mean. Let's use our example of the item that costs $1.00. We learned that with a 33.33% margin our sell price would be $1.50 and our margin would be 50 cents. If we effectively lowered our cost to 90 cents and still assigned a 33.33% margin to it we would then have a retail price of $1.35 and realize profit of only 45 cents. The only reason you'd ever want to do this is if you were not currently priced competitively.

Now let's assume that you kept the retail price the same at $1.50 and used the lowered cost of 90 cents. You would now realize a profit of 60 cents which would represent a 40% margin. That would be a very nice improvement. Let's get real here, though. You probably won't lower your costs by 10% just by combining purchases. It will probably be more likely in the 1/2-2% range, but the lesson is still sound.

3. <u>Round up.</u> Rounding up is the process of taking computed retails to a predetermined higher point. For example, let's say that you have computed your retail price for a product and it comes to 13.02. You might have predetermined that you would take every price to the nearest 9. So, in this case, your retail price would become 13.09 instead of 13.02.

There are also systems that round to the next higher .25 so in this case the price might become 13.25. A system like this produces incremental increases and incremental increases at the end of the year can be very powerful. The critical point is to have your key employees in the loop as to what you expect so that they can implement the plan when prices are computed. If you're already using a primary vendor and they either furnish you with price tags or upload information into your point of sale it's a good bet that they can help you with rounding.

4. <u>Don't price individual items.</u> For those of you doing this already it will seem to be a no-brainer. For those of you who are still putting price tags on every item it is important that you understand all of the advantages this simple change could afford.

I am suggesting that instead of pricing individual items you simply put up bin tags that display your prices. There is the obvious advantage of the time savings realized by not applying individual tags. Remember time saved is payroll cut so that, in and of itself, is very advantageous. But beyond that you can instantly change prices by changing the retail in your point-of-sale and your bin tag.

If you learn that an item's cost is increasing, you can raise your retail price instantly. You won't have to peel tags or place a higher retail price over a lower one, which can make you look shady. Instead you'll have clean packaging and instantaneous margin protection.

5. <u>Margin incentive bonuses.</u> Because yearly incremental raises can adversely affect your business in coming years you may find it advantageous to make pay increases in the form of bonuses. With this type of system, the payroll numbers will only increase as business does. Then, in the case of downturns, you won't find yourself with crippling payroll percentages.

    A great foundation for this type of system is to tie the bonus structure to margins. There are a couple of advantages. Employees are much more tuned-in to protecting your margin when it benefits them personally. Often systems tied to only volume fail to do this and, in fact, can complicate margins even further. We have written for several of our customers spread sheets that allow them to explore how they might structure a system and then to communicate it to the employees.

    A margin-based incentive plan can be implemented individually or collectively. We have noticed when employees are "coupled" in this fashion they begin to work together and occasionally even exert peer pressure on each other when good numbers are not being achieved.

6. <u>Private brands.</u> There are many national branded products that, due to their market penetration, produce poor margins. You may learn that you can find a private labeled brand of equivalent product, or

depending on your company's size, even produce your own.

I have seen some studies that showed that people were moving back to national brands because of quality issues. That makes it imperative that if you show private brands that quality control be sterling. You are tying your store's reputation to each product you sell.

A good strategy is to show the national brand for those who will accept nothing else, while showing the private branded product at an attractively lower price. The key point is whether the private branded product can be sold at a lower price and yet still produce good margin. If such is not true, there would really be no advantage to it.

As an aside, but slightly off subject, you must maintain items for customers to compare to. For example if you are selling a kitchen counter mixer set for $198 and that is the only one you're stocking you'll probably experience slow sales. Add another model that sells for $298 and you'll find that you'll sell both models. It is the simple fact that your shoppers can now compare and choose between this model and that. They will feel like educated shoppers because they have considered more than one alternative. Try it.

7. <u>Special order pricing.</u> It is time to review how you price special order items. Many retailers think that they must be hyper-competitive on special orders. However, there are two important considerations here. (1) The customer may have looked high and low and been unable to find the item in-stock locally and now is faced with special-ordering it somewhere. Their quest may have taken them to several stops and they are now just ready to make a decision and get it behind them. I'm not suggesting that you gouge, under any circumstances. It's just that often times we find retailers who think that if they don't have the item in-stock they don't "deserve" their regular margin. I believe that the regular margin + 5-8% for the extra steps involved represents a good starting point. You should review your procedures and determine if this will work for you. (2) Often your store is selected to place the special order simply because of your convenience to the shopper. Convenience is worth a premium.

8. <u>Up-selling and suggestive selling.</u> Up selling refers to processes by which sales staff guides customers to products which have higher retail prices. Suggestive selling is similar but involves recommending items that would go well with the primary purchase. When we are training store staffs we often find that employees, for different reasons, have aversions to these processes.

Failing to perform these critical functions can kill margin and volume. Higher ticket items should produce more margin dollars. Sell more premium items and your margin will increase. Simply because the tags are higher, so too will be the collective volume.

Suggestive selling will not necessarily increase margin (it can though) but will definitely increase sales.

Why then this aversion to performing these important tasks? We believe it to be two different issues. In the case of up-selling we have interviewed employees and have determined that many of them do what we now refer to a "personal-economic casting". This involves an employee looking at the higher price and filtering it through their own financial situation. If they couldn't afford to buy the item they instinctively steer the customer toward something lower in price.

Beyond this, however, is the stereo-typical salesperson image represented by the caricature of a used car salesperson. Some employees just don't want to be a pain to their customers and they view up-selling or suggestive-selling in that light.

We have found training using different labels to be helpful. For example we train using "actively assisting" to describe suggestive selling and "possibility exploration" instead of up selling. People who have aversions to the "S" words seem to find these descriptors to be more palatable.

9. <u>Merchandising</u>. We've already discussed how proper merchandising can increase your store's margin. I don't want to repeat it, but I do want to underscore the importance of good merchandising as it affects stores' margins.

10. <u>Controlling discounts.</u> We have witnessed operations in which employees had the ability to discount at their discretion in order to "close" deals. Unfortunately, in this type of atmosphere, sometimes discounting becomes the first path of action instead of a last.

    Beyond this remember to stay cognizant of mark-down discounts too. Several steps of discounting to close out merchandise are preferable to one deep discount. By using several steps you'll maintain incremental margin advantages.

11. <u>Advertising.</u> This is another point that we have discussed already. It bears reinforcement in a topic on store margin. Remember the key is guiding customers to buy add-ons to your advertised items. This is done through communicative signage and employee education.

12. Product mix. The 80/20 rule comes in to play in many areas of retail. For example, as a rule of thumb, 20% of your products will produce 80% of your sales. The enigma is that if you closed out the other 80% you'd find that the 80/20 rule would still apply. Beyond that you'd soon find your product mix to be so anemic that your store would no longer attract customers.

    The items that are more obscure and produce fewer sales must also produce greater margins. This takes us back to the beginning of this week's study and the importance of having a variable pricing system in place.

13. Ask. Many retailers price their merchandise without being aware of what competitors are doing. After you complete the price shops covered earlier in this week's strategy, and when you find opportunity, price those items higher.

    This once again varies a great deal with store slotting. If your store is slotted as a convenience store (see Discovery-Based Retail, A Slot for Success) you can and must have higher retail prices and operating margins.

Pricing, price image, and margin are critical variables to store operations. Study this week's information and spend time understanding and planning better results.

8. Short-term and long-term planning

Whether your company is new and finding its way, or established and already successful, it is important to set both short-term and long-term goals. Honest analysis of one's company is not always easy. However, it is an important step in strategizing for the future.

You may find it helpful to begin the process with a S.W.O.T. evaluation. S.W.O.T. is an acronym for strengths, weaknesses, opportunities, and threats. From this point forward I'll refer to this system as swot, and validate the word in my spell checker so it doesn't drive me mad.

Historically, with this type of strategizing process, strengths and weaknesses are often viewed as internal attributes, while opportunities and threats are viewed as external factors.

We find it advantageous, however, to examine all four quadrants both extrinsically and intrinsically. To perform the latter forces examination of in-house systems and procedures, which we feel is a great use of time. Of course, identifying weaknesses, opportunities or threats are of little value without strategies to either capitalize on or minimize the effects of the revelations.

You'll often see the process represented by a box with 4 quadrants as below. As I mentioned and as the columns are labeled, in the left column you would list what you perceive to be your operations' strengths and weaknesses, typically internal attributes. The right column would hold the external or extrinsic factors that you might designate as opportunities or threats.

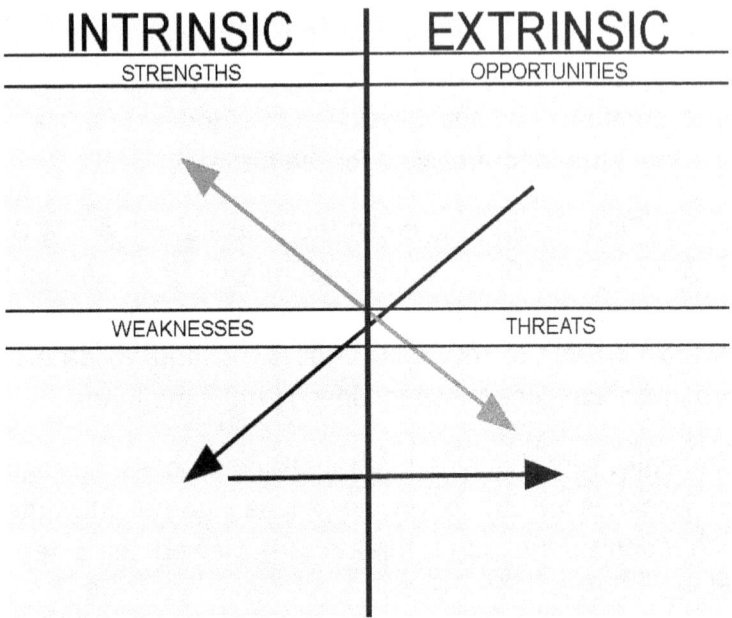

The analytical process by itself is a waste of time. The process coupled with real strategizing sessions to address what you discover is very valuable and can be the springboard to greatness.

I'll explain how this might work, which will also allow me to explain the reciprocals that you'll become aware of as you work through the process.

Let's say that you sit down with key staff members and discuss what you view as the strengths of your organization.

Within the course of that discussion you decide to list experienced reliable personnel as strength.

With that attribute listed as strength, consider the time ramifications. How long, in your best estimate, will that remain strength? Perhaps two key employees are slated to retire within the next five years. At the end of that period, what is now a listed strength may not remain so, without sufficient planning to assure that it does.

Glance at the chart again. I have drawn a line arrow from the upper left hand quadrant (strength) to the lower right (threat) to indicate that we need, within our longer term plan, to address a current strength that will have a terminal point. The fact that the current strength has a terminal point establishes that it may become a threat. This reciprocal relationship of quadrants is a main reason I feel that intrinsic and extrinsic elements should be analyzed together.

Let's consider another hypothetical situation. Your store is currently doing well. You've heard through the grapevine that a competitor's store in an adjacent market might be coming up for sale within the next five years. In your planning you would likely list that revelation in the upper right quadrant as an opportunity.

Now, refer back to the drawing. I represented reciprocal relationships with the solid arrow line. I first drew a solid line from upper right to lower left. Even though the opportunity may present itself, would we have sufficient resources to capitalize? If not, that would represent a long-term weakness. When examining that as a possibility, it causes us to consider who might take advantage of the opportunity if we're unable to. Perhaps it will be an owner who is more aggressive than the current ones. If that should happen it would represent a threat.

In this case, the strategic thinking and planning has taken us three quarters of the way around the chart. It has drawn to our attention an opportunity that could, without much stretch of our imagination, turn in to a threat.

Our short and mid-term planning might include provisions for how we could earmark funds for the next few years to act on the opportunity should it arise as we expect. If it doesn't, we'll have some extra capital for other opportunities; if it does we'll come off as champs due to our superior strategic planning.

Make an exhaustive list of items that fall within each quadrant. Before you start formulating your strategies, however, it's a good idea to pare them to the ones that you consider to be the most critical. This will allow you to plan more specificity into your short-term and long-term goals.

Another note of caution: Managers and owners assess their stores differently than do their customers. Remember that you must balance the opposite ends of a teeter-totter, one end representing profitability and the other, customer interface. Therefore, it might be a great time to solicit opinions from your customers.

We have now performed our swot analysis and have come up with both short term and long term plans and goals. We are missing an important component. Without specific deadlines for incremental steps, it is unlikely that our goals will be achieved.

Here's a suggestion as to how you can use Excel to help you schedule incremental steps. The beauty of using this is that you have flexibility in moving up or back your completion date. Take a look at the following picture and then I'll explain what it represents.

ENTER DESIRED COMPLETION DATE	9/15/13
STEP 1	9/20/12
STEP 2	12/9/12
STEP 3	1/18/13

You'll notice that I've plugged in a completion date of 9/15/13. I did not code hard dates for the incremental steps. I formatted those cells to hold date values and then compute "completion date – 360 days, 280 days and 240 days, respectively. If I choose to change the project completion date, each of the incremental step deadlines will be recomputed automatically.

In the picture below, I changed the completion date to December of 2014 and you'll see that all of the incremental step dates have been recalculated.

ENTER DESIRED COMPLETION DATE	12/15/14
STEP 1	12/20/13
STEP 2	3/10/14
STEP 3	4/19/14

This is certainly not rocket-science or even cutting-edge programming, but it is a very practical use of Excel which can help you monitor incremental steps for larger tasks.

A couple more columns on this sheet would make sense. One column would designate whose primary responsibility was the assigned task and the other simply a completed date check-off.

I mentioned earlier, but it bears repeating that identifying the issues is meaningless without formulating a plan to address them.

9. Watching and working the numbers

Most retailers turn their bookkeeping over to professionals who are paid and trained to handle the numbers. However, it just makes sense to better understand the calculations and ratios that affect your bottom line.

Our company developed a system we call The Profit Explorer which we use to coach retailers regarding budgeting and their P&Ls. It has been startling to get an inside glimpse of how many store owners seem to expect the numbers to just happen.

During this week's discussion we'll look at some important equations that will help you analyze your operation and compare it to industry benchmarks.

Let's start with some simple ones.

- Gross margin refers to the dollar amount realized from sales. It is simple to compute.
    - Gross margin = Sales – cost of goods sold.

The reason this simple equation is worth consideration is that gross margin dollars are different from gross margin percentage. You will have a gross margin percentage target number. However, sometimes, you may have an opportunity to close a large sale that would produce less than the percentage goal. You would then have to consider the gross margin dollars you would gain and decide if it made sense to proceed.

- Gross margin percentage refers to the percentage of a sale (or sales) that is realized as profit.
    - Gross Margin % = (Sales $ - Cost of Goods $)/Sales$

Example $500 sale - $300 Cost of goods = $200 divided by $500 = 40% Gross Margin.

This is a critical number, whether drilled down to individual transactions or evaluated for the year. The number as a single calculation has little meaning without comparing it to the same calculation over a period of time (are my margins getting better) or evaluated against industry benchmarks.

Gross margin percentage varies widely from industry to industry. For example, reports place the hardware industry average at around 39%-41%. Apparel stores can run near 50%, while audio-video stores will operate in the lower 30% range.

- G.M.R.O.I. is an acronym for "gross margin return on inventory" This is a critical ratio that spotlights the gross margin returned for every inventory dollar invested.
    - GMROI = Gross margin $ ÷ Avg. Inventory @ Cost

Note that unlike the first two equations which were extracted from the P&L, this one will require both the P&L and your balance sheet. (The inventory information will come from the balance sheet.)

A simplified way of computing average inventory is adding beginning and ending inventories and dividing by two. If your inventory stays relatively consistent, this simple calculation will work fine.

If your inventory varies during the year, a more accurate figure can be derived by adding the first day of year inventory, and each end of month inventory over the total year and dividing by 13. (You'll divide by thirteen because you'll have two inventory figures the first month of your fiscal year, the first and last day of the month.)

A higher number for GMROI is more desirable, of course, but targets will vary by industry. For example recent numbers indicated that the average GMROI for furniture stores was $2.50 while convenience store produced slightly over $6.00. Remember to compare to benchmarks within your industry.

- Return on assets, ROA measures the productivity of all assets.
    - Net Income ÷ average assets.

Like, GMROI, with ROA we desire a higher number. We want a bigger return on our investment in assets. To calculate your ROA will require both your balance sheet and your income statement.

Now let's examine a calculation which will return a number called Current ratio.

- Current ratio indicates if a company is positioned to meet its short-term debt obligations.
    - Current assets ÷ Current liabilities = Current ratio.

Like other indicators we've examined, current ratios will vary between industries. However, a current ratio of 2 – 3 indicates that a company is likely to be able to meet its short-term obligations. E.g. 12 months

- A stricter test of liquidity involves a calculation termed "quick ratio". The quick ratio equation uses only the most liquid assets as seen below.
    - Quick ratio = Cash + Accounts Receivable ÷ Current liabilities.

Because only the most liquid assets are calculated, this number will be lower than current ratio. A quick ratio will usually average between .5 and 2, but this ratio must be analyzed carefully.

Higher is typically better, but, if accounts receivables have ballooned above normal levels, this could create high Quick Ratios, masking other problems. Businesses that typically pay cash, and have little or no receivables, (think restaurants) can have low Quick Ratios but not be credit risks.

I mentioned that high Quick Ratios are desirable...usually. Ballooning receivables are dangerous and in certain industries can quickly cripple an enterprise. For example, building materials dealers, who regularly work on narrow margins due to their competitive environment, can find themselves crippled by slow pay. There are computations that can monitor the time element of payables. These numbers will come from your balance sheet.

- Average collection period (days on the books) is an indicator of how long it is taking a retailer to turn receivables in to cash.
    - Average collection period = Average Accounts Receivable ÷ (Credit Annual Sales ÷ 365)

The result of this equation will be a number that represents days. Let's look at an example. Joe's Lumber has annual credit sales of $650,000. His average accounts receivable over a calendar year is $56,000. Average accounts receivable are figured by taking month's end receivables for each month, adding them together and dividing by 12.

His credit yearly sales of $650,000 divided by 365 equals (we'll round up) 1781. This result divided by his average accounts receivable number of $56,000 equals 31.44. Therefore, on average it takes him 31 days to turn his receivables into cash. It should be Joe's goal to make incremental improvements on this variable.

Average collection period is a number that needs to be compared within your specific industry and, probably even more important, to itself over time. Comparing to industry can give you a benchmark, but comparison to self will monitor improvement. Set yourself specific goals based on your current results and commit to lowering the number.

I stated earlier that we often find payroll to be a big culprit in struggling businesses. Depending on your industry, of course, I would say failure to successfully collect receivables in a timely manner would run close second.

- You'll often hear or read that a company's sales are up or down by a percentage over last year. Here is the formula for determining your sales increase or decrease over another period.
  - (This period's sales $ - Last period's sales $) / Last period's sales dollars.

This equation will return a percentage comparison to the last period and is helpful to serve as a gage of progress or regression.

Of course, sales will vary with the economy, weather and other extrinsic factors. To successfully account for these variables, take sales from a five-year period and calculate how much each month contributed to the year, historically.

For example, you may find that January contributed 5.8% of the year's sales over the course of 5 years while March may have contributed 8.3%. After you have calculated these percentages you can compare this month's results against your year's goal. You'll then know how your store performed against goal using historic reference points.

Another critical variable that you should be aware of is inventory turns. Simply stated, inventory turns represent the number of time you "sell through" and replace your inventory during the year.
- o Inventory turns = Cost of Goods Sold ÷ Average Inventory @ Cost

This is another number that will vary by industry. Higher is better, but there are cautions here too. If your inventory turns are much higher than industry averages it could signal that you are missing sales due to insufficient stock. This would be corrected by raising reorder quantities, if you're noticing out-of-stocks at reorder.

Low inventory turns can signal other problems including holding obsolete product. If your inventory turns are low, carefully evaluate as to possible causes. Of course, there will be seasonal variations during periods you are purposely holding higher inventories... e.g. preparing for holidays or other special promotions. If that is not the case with your low number then consider how to pare inventory to a range that will produce normal turns within your industry.

We'll take a look at one last formula.
- o Debt to worth ratio = Total Liabilities ÷ Total Owner's equity.

These numbers, which will come from the balance sheet, effectively measure the financial strength of a company by contrasting what it owes against what it owns.

A Dr. orders a patient's blood drawn to evaluate its different elements. He can then determine which of the components are not in normal ranges. Depending on what he finds, he will begin to consider reasons for the abnormal markers. Once he hypothesizes a reason for the abnormalities he will prescribe a course of treatment. If his hypothesis is correct the patient will improve. If not, the patient will stay the same or become more ill. The Dr. will repeat this process (it is practicing medicine isn't it?) until he correctly diagnoses the ailment.

This is not unlike the process that astute managers undertake with the numbers we have outlined in this week's exercise.

Without specific "normal" ranges for blood test markers, the Dr. would be "winging it", and only guessing at what ailed his patient. Without industry reports and averages, the calculations we discussed would be similarly impotent. However, just as in the medical examination, your examination of your store's numbers can give great insights as to the health of your business and steps you could take to make it better.

Here's one last word of caution. Just as a thorough medical examination should occur regularly, so too should the examination of your store's numbers. You can think of your accountant as a "specialist" and yourself as a general practitioner. Don't leave the analysis solely to him or her. Repeat the calculations until you understand them and can interpret what they mean to you and your store's success.

10. Systems, Processes and Tying it Altogether

There are systems and processes within your store that probably date back to its beginnings. Many of them may still be sound. That having been said, however, being sound, and being optimal, are not necessarily the same.

The simplest tasks that your staff completes may hold opportunities for time savings. If time is saved, it is freed for other tasks. If time is freed and managed properly, either productivity goes up or payroll goes down. Either way, you win. Beyond time, there may be changes to processes which could ensure greater accuracy, or better customer experience.

I mentioned in the opening of this book that I have affixed a name to continuing those things which we are originally taught. "Retail genetics" is a good self-defining characterization of transmitting, through the years, retail operational habits, both good and bad.

The reason I think this worth pointing out is that once a system is in place and working reasonably well, it is seldom questioned. Systems which are never questioned may hold wonderful opportunities for improvement.

There has been no guide, at least to my knowledge, of how one might go about this task. So let's discuss a way in which it might happen.

If you've ever studied diets you've probably noticed one of the common recommendations is to write down everything you consume. The rationale for this very effective process is that it tunes the mind into exactly what is causing and maintaining weight gain. For example the keeper of such a journal might learn that they are not consuming great quantities, but be shocked to learn how bad their food mix is. Others would be startled at how much they actually do "pig out".

What if you were to, for a period of time, manage your staff's time consumption in a similar fashion? I'm not talking about a month or year. I don't want you to waste time, learning how you might save some. However, I do think it would be appropriate to ask each of your employees to document, in 15 minute increments, how they spend their day for a week or two.

As an example, perhaps Bill will show that he spends 3 hours on Wednesday checking in freight. Joe indicates he spends 3 hours helping Bill.

Depending on the critical aspect of time in getting the order to the floor, it's possible that if Bill and Joe each took the full responsibility on alternate weeks, they could actually complete the task in less than the collective 6 hours. We might find that by assigning the task to one, you would prevent "visiting time" and also set up friendly competition as to who completes the task quickest during their appointed week.

Another possible result of the same examination is that when you consider the number of vendor errors or shortages that were discovered, and weigh those against the costs, you might conclude that you'd be money ahead to skip the check-in process and move the freight directly to the sales floor.

Of course, this is a simple example and represents a small store. In your store, and depending on its scope of operation, it will be necessary to review the week's journals from your employees and then formulate strategies to experiment with the opportunities you discover.

You might find, for instance, that because of a focus on cross-training, your staff seems to have no clear understanding on what their responsibilities actually are. If so, it might bring about greater awareness and need for new job descriptions.

Simply by asking employees to complete this process will shake up their world and have them considering for themselves how productive they actually are. You'll also have them guessing about what you're up to. That might be kind of fun...unh?

I shopped a store recently which is a single location of a very successful chain of hardware stores in this area. The store has an awkward layout with almost no decompression zone. I had taken five steps into their environment when a young man asked if he could help me.

It felt very awkward to me. I hadn't been in before and I didn't know what products they carried. After he interrupted my transitional space, I did tell him what I was looking for, and as it turns out, they didn't stock "gas fire pits". I asked if they could special order one as I was in no particular hurry. He told me he would have to ask the manager. He made the call, went to their electronic catalog, and then had to call the manager again to get a pass word.

There were a number of break-downs that occurred as a result of retail genetics. I'm sure that this store prides itself on customer service and translates good customer service to be greeting customers quickly and leading them to whatever product they might be looking for. That is a very outdated traditional view and one that needs to be reviewed.

Unfortunately this young man had not been trained to respect a decompression area nor had he been trained sufficiently in something as simple as helping a customer peruse a special order catalog.

If each customer were greeted as quickly as I was, there were too many people keyed on this. Recent studies have shown that personal contact with a sales person is no longer the primary interpretation of good "customer service". Rather merchandise in stock, pleasant environments and pricing were all characterized as part of the customer service experience by today's shoppers.

Because he greeted me so soon, I wasn't exposed to other products that I may have found while looking for gas fire pits. Because of the store's procedures, I knew, from three steps in, that they didn't have any.

A simple "Welcome to our store, let us know if you need some help" after I was there for a few minutes would have been a much more productive approach.

If time journaling had been conducted in this store, the employee might have written that he spent the entire day helping customers. After comparing his notes against transaction numbers however, the manager would probably have learned that the staff member's day was spent just waiting for the next customer. The process could reveal opportunity for better utilization of resources.

He could be assigned the primary task of maintaining a section of the store, taught to greet customers later in their shopping experience and everybody would win.

I could imagineer other hypothetical results of time journaling a store. It would have little value, however, because there are so many variables. Let your creative juices flow now and consider how you might use the process to make more money for your store and yourself.

10 Weeks to a Better Retail Operation

Final thoughts

Your biggest challenge to complete these processes will be stepping outside of yourself and your environment to make honest assessments.

You can do it. You can use this information to improve your store or reengineer it completely. If you would like help we offer a program that we call the "Two-day tune-up" which is an in-store consult program. We also offer a "by-phone" consult that is even more cost effective. On our websites you will also find tools and tons of additional information that will help you with your quest for improved performance.

Our company's websites are discoverybasedretail.com and discoverdbr.com

Thanks for reading "*10 Weeks to a Better Retail Operation.*" You would also enjoy and learn from the book Discovery-Based Retail.

10 Weeks to a Better Retail Operation

www.ingramcontent.com/pod-product-compliance
Lightning Source LLC
Chambersburg PA
CBHW061509180526
45171CB00001B/105